The New

Spirituality

Food For Thought

Diet

*Lose:

~ Fear, Low Self Esteem, Negative Thinking, Worry, Blame &
Limiting Beliefs!

*Gain:

~ Happiness, Self love, Inner Peace, The Meaning of Life ~

~ A "no-nonsense" ~

~ SIMPLIFIED manual for spiritual growth ~

~ A seekers - must-have ! ~

David A. Rench

Sudio Press

First Edition 2016 ©

www.newspiritualitydiet.com

CONGRATULATIONS

If you have stumbled upon this book, I am happy for you.
I welcome you with open arms, as it is a sign of synchronicity
that a new spiritual happening is most likely in your future.
Congratulations on your readiness to join the ever growing
spiritual healing of mankind and absorb the information and
techniques found within these pages.
This is reason to celebrate, gain freedoms,
become insightful and be grateful!
Please remember that this manual has been written not to
change your mind but to give you the tools and insights to learn
how to change your own mind.
I bid you peace.

Dedication:

Dedicated to my spiritual growth partner and wife, Carol Cibira Rench and to my children Rebecca and Adam. A huge THANK YOU and love back atcha to my guides, higher self and Source for all the helpful communication since I was a child. Also to my mother Amelia for paving the journey to the understanding of contrasts and to my father Martin Rench who left my life too early and left a hole that only sadness emanated from until I realized the potential for love that was its near opposite.

A huge thank you to Teresa of Avila for my lesson in vibrational loss, when judgment is involved.

I want to express my appreciation for the artwork illustrations created by Indiana Rench, River Rench and Finn Johnson.

Thanks for the use of Matthew Johnson's flower garden for the cover inspiration and Rebecca Johnson's input and continued exploration into natural healing methodology.

I am also grateful for Moss Johnson's willingness to listen and all of my spiritually inclined friends around the globe.

Huge thanks to Adam M. Rench our physical guidance counselor and for helping me see options with the content of Chapter 39 "Life's Equation".

Thank you to Linda Rench for her willingness to be a positive sounding board and have an open mind.

I appreciate the input on cover design from Linda Oeffling and I offer great big thanks to Lynda Jo Nordstrom and Jennifer McVey for their greatly appreciated input and proof reading efforts!

May you all find inner peace and walk with the force.

"The two most important days of your life are the day you were born and the day you find out why!"

~ Mark Twain

Introduction

As Paulo Coelho says in <u>The Alchemist</u> "It's the possibility of a dream come true that makes life interesting." This book is about life's process. Using the information and techniques outlined in this book, you will begin to understand that you too can arrive at a place in your mind that will allow such an inspired life. The books contents offer an option to the mundane. The secrets revealed can give you the right to choose one of life's more positive outcomes. A wondrous life can unfold, rather than having to die with your opus buried within.

We are not born with our inner make up. Our purpose has been foreseen but our inner unrest is not in our genes. As we grow, we fill our clean newborn mental slate by absorption. We are taught by words, actions, and beliefs from influential events in our life. Other beliefs are not taught as they are adopted thru osmosis from our parents, relatives and culture.

These false beliefs are energies around us and as a result become fuel for the developing false self or ego. These beliefs are the foundations of our life's adventures and challenges, which are actually powerful future opportunities for inner growth.

As adults we don't have to blindly accept the pain and unrest fueled by these untruths. Read the contents of this book and come join me on an inner adventure. Hidden wonders and a new level of inner peace await your arrival.

"Your task is not to seek for love, but merely to seek and find all the barriers within yourself that you have built against it"

~ Rumi

11

FORWARD

I began this manual for my own use as I started my spiritual journey. I needed a reference to prevent me from mentally slipping backwards as I took in the new and swept out the old. It was sometimes difficult for me to remember everything I was experiencing and learning. As I approached my internal makeup and began the positive evolution of it's contents, I read and re-read this manual many, many times. When the manual neared completion it was difficult to give birth to the physical book, as my revelations and subsequent growth were happening quickly. Revisions were added often. As I proofed the book and re-read it's contents, I continued to learn from my own entries. I now offer it to you in hopes that it can offer you the same freedoms I discovered. When we begin a spiritual journey and become a seeker of truth, we begin to identify the controlling fearful beliefs and thoughts that don't offer us inner peace. As we learn how to separate from fear we start to shed these false layers of belief like an onion, one layer at a time. These layers of falseness are discarded as we experience truthful revelations, "ah ha" moments and jumps through the Satori window (Satori = Japanese Buddhist term for awakening). As the layers peel away, we gain freedoms as we discard the less than loving thoughts and make room for the new. With the new, come truths, more freedoms, and consequently one's energy expands, simultaneously generating happiness plus a higher personal vibration or inner level of energy. That higher vibration grows our soul's strength and the layers of the onion continue to fall away to reveal a hidden flower bud within, which slowly allows a beautiful blossom to open. The blossom was always there, we are not bad, broken or flawed, we just couldn't see its potential. The false ego self had it hidden from view. That blossom was obscured from our consciousness by the adopted beliefs, egoic layers of insecurities, doubts, life's challenges, painful emotions and judgments. The seed that allows euphoric feelings of peace and love is waiting to be discovered and always existed within each and every one of us. That latent seed, the true Holy Grail, needs only to be found and allowed positive food to grow. You see, the peace, the truths, the longings we search for are never without, they are always discovered within.

13

Authors note:

At this time you do not have to believe in God for many of the following concepts to work for you. Personally I use the words: God, The Force, Source, Higher Self, The Divine, The Powers That Be, Great Spirit and the Universe as interchangeable descriptive words to describe God. When you come across one of these words, please use whatever word is most comfortable for you. Since God is all loving, magnanimous, and defies description, he/she won't mind which word you choose.

Please allow my occasional redundancy. It was of my opinion that some key methods and interpretations were important enough to mention more than once.

Namaste,
David A. Rench

"Yesterday I was clever, so I wanted to change the world. Today I am wise, so I am changing myself."

~ Rumi

❧Chapter One❧

The Beginning:

When we are born, we all enter this Earth-plane level of physical existence with a purpose. An imaginary clipboard of sorts upon which is written our life's goal. We all have connections to The Divine, as helpers guide us toward the fulfillment of our purpose, but it is with the use of free will that we make our choices, which determine the rapidity and full extent of accomplishing that purpose. Guides are spiritual entities and are often called guardian angels. These guides are souls who have crossed over and spiritually evolved to a point where they can now offer guidance from the other side. Other familiar terms for the other side are heaven, spirit world or you might say, a different level of mind. Our helpers guide us in many ways such as intuition, a gut feeling, or voice in the head, keeping us from harm and often steering us toward seemingly random moments which can offer the possibility of a shorter path toward the completion of the contents of our clipboard. These guides have experienced many past physical lives and have evolved to a point where they evolve even more by helping someone in the physical. The ultimate reason for incarnation (born into a life experience on Earth) is to grow our higher-self, of which we are only a part. We detach from that higher-self with little memory of our total magnificence to not only grow ourselves, but as we do so, to grow God. As Eckhart Tolle wrote in The Power of Now, "You are here to enable the divine purpose of the universe to unfold. That is how important you are."

Many of the key people we meet while in the physical (parents, family members, spouse, lovers, close friends, enemies, etc.) also have a life purpose and have previously agreed to a destiny to enter our experience, before incarnation. Many of the opportunities, which will offer us the most growth possibility, are predetermined in conjunction with these key people who will enter our lives. You more than likely have had previous incarnations with the same people you are close to in this lifetime. When you are guided into a life situation and react out of fear, you have just been given an opportunity to change that reaction to one based out of love. This is where free will comes into play. It is your choice to heal by adopting a loving approach or continue to react from an internal fear, thus remaining in a more troubled mindset. Many of our internal beliefs are based on fear. It is our internal beliefs that each of us can challenge, to find a loving alternative. If you look back upon your past it is quite likely that you will remember the key moments that offered the opportunity for change. These situations will be more vivid in your mind and more easily remembered. There will seemingly be quite a bit of useless filler in between those moments but that filler is more than likely allowing you to wallow in a situation that would quickly change if you could alter the mindset that placed you there in the first place. This time spent in a situation that isn't in your best interest often seems like a waste but is actually what I call hell. Hell, because you are not healing from within and you are stagnating in discomfort.

As we confront our learning opportunities with intentions, thoughts, and actions, free will offers us the choice to react with

17

response based on a "fearful thought" or a "loving thought." Negative reaction always has its origin from fearful thought. Several examples of fear-based reactions are hate, revenge, guilt, worry, worthlessness, judgment, revenge, violence, blame and victimization. When you heal an internal fear-based thought by adopting a new positive loving thought from within, you have gained a freedom and helped raise your energy level. The raising of your energy is a gift you experience, as you simultaneously share it with everyone else. All energies are derived from one Source, are vibrational and contribute to attracting similar energies, as we continue on our journey. This higher loving energy level is your offering, as it raises the level of human consciousness and helps others to do the same. The awareness of this process is a step toward enlightenment, as it solves the elusive debate on why some people have good or bad luck. When your energy experiences a journey to a higher level, it is not a coincidence that your luck also changes for the better. An example of this would be a person who has adopted a thought system based on being a victim. This "woe is me" victim consciousness will be the force behind that which gets reflected back to that person in the form of experiences, which will offer opportunities for personal growth. Since our outer world is a reflection of our inner world, the type of experiences offered a victim can be seen as negative until they are, with the use of loving change, deemed opportunities for eliminating the victim consciousness. Self-love is one of the keys to walking toward inner peace and if you are a victim (within your mind) you will be prone to accidents, cars not performing perfectly, a lack of money, mental angst, frustration, depression, etc. Change the victim thought pattern, increase your self-love and you will consequently change your life experiences. This system of evolution is a never ending growth process and when embraced as such, is a process that will be consciously sped up or slowed down based on the strength of one's character to endure life's progression. It has been said that God gives those with more character, more difficult tasks (growth opportunity) here on Earth.

The secondary experiences we encounter are all useful but all really either point toward completion of our main purpose or

18

how easily we endorse the fears that keep us from it's completion. Discovering our life's purpose is one of the most important blessings you can discover. While in my 30's, I was told by a psychic that the main reason for my incarnation was to experience male energy and have the opportunity to become comfortable being a man. I had put that information in my back pocket and never forgot it but did not give it full credence until decades later. Looking back on my life, retrospection revealed that there were challenges from birth that offered fuel for growth to understand male energy. I was the third son born to a woman who desperately wanted a daughter. Unable to give birth to a fourth child resulted in my mother being disappointed that I wasn't female. She not only blamed me for her future life without a daughter and a subsequent hysterectomy, but sometimes treated me like a daughter. Life challenge number one was to grow up being confident as a boy and as I grew older, a man. Unaware of my mission, I tackled it with a lack of confidence, especially toward the opposite sex. The girls loved me when I was 5, 6 and 7 years old. I can remember running away from them on the school playground and joked in my later years about being disappointed when they all didn't do the same when I became a teen. This lack of confidence was evident during my later grade school years as I remember having several girlfriends before I had the courage to kiss one of them. That first kiss with Laura was a turning point and thoroughly is etched into my mind. Being overly sensitive, while testing the waters of life and as continued insecurities filled my mind, I progressed through my remaining grade school days.

Contemplations at an early age found me in thought about the permanent nature of death. These thoughts were frequent and I remember thinking about rotting in the ground and having no thought, after death. I don't know if this is a common thought pattern for a young child, but I like to think these thoughts laid a foundation for finding answers that were to come later in life.

My father worked most nights and became terminally ill when I was quite young. Because of such, I was lacking in a constant positive male role model. During this time period, my mother was afraid of my growing independence as I tested my growing masculinity. She wasn't sure she could properly raise me

19

without my father. This fearful parental mindset created a situation that is vivid in my mind as I remember a day while in my late grade school years. At a friend's house, I asserted my masculine energy when I challenged a bully who was bothering us. Until I started to lose this physical fight, the situation was a great opportunity to take a step toward being comfortable as a man. Before the fight was over, my mother drove up, found us fighting and broke up the altercation. She drove me home and beat me with a belt simultaneously screaming that I should never fight again. My reaction was to take this beating without emotion, wall up my anger and carry this emotional scar from the experience into my adulthood. A rebel was born.

My father passed away just after my 17th birthday. Trauma from that experience was piled onto the others. I remember not having any questions answered, concerning my fathers passing. It was understood that we would all deal with this on our own. Since I was quite young, it was difficult to deal with any healing approach for coping with the loss of my father. I remember going into the funeral home for a family only, open casket viewing. My father had asked for a closed casket, requesting such before he died. It was his opinion that if anyone wanted to see him, they would had visited him before he died. At that family open casket experience, the shock of the reality of what had happened to my father began to set in. I was frozen, standing there witness to the lifeless body of my father in the casket. I remember being pushed forward by my Aunt. At that moment of being pushed forward, the experience somehow symbolized I had to accept the reality of what I was experiencing. My mind couldn't accept that situation and I lost consciousness. I remember opening my eyes looking up at many faces as a vial was being held under my nose. It was very unpleasant and as I awoke they took that vial of what I now assume was smelling salts away. I think of that moment as a defining moment. I was angry with my aunt for pushing me forward into a situation that I was not ready to absorb and I closed up. I had put a wall around my heart, assuming that if I didn't love another; I could never be hurt if something happened to them. This unconscious mental decision was to be a nemesis and a mental trait I was to slowly dissolve over the future decades of my life. I lived at home but was pretty much on my own. I dated other girls but over a period of three years, always returned to date Carol, my future wife. There were driving forces, which I now know were strong karmic energies that finally found us getting married. We were going to be offered many lessons. My wife and I married at a young age and during our first nine years of marriage lacked the ability to use meaningful communication. Unbeknownst to us, we both harbored low internal self value systems, poor communication skills and reacted to life's trials based on our internal makeup. As we experienced our learning situations, difficulties and failures, as many do, we concluded that the disappointing and painful situations we manifested were happening due to bad luck. We blamed each other, other people and the world around us for what was happening to us. As a result, we hurt each other with our words and actions to a point that we both started seeing other people. You may be familiar with the saying the grass is always greener on the other side. What this common saying means is as humans we often conclude that other circumstances seem more desirable than one's current situation. The first action is to run away from or choose a new situation. Those new circumstances are never the solution and rarely better then the initial situation. What that saying is trying to convey is that many people take the seemingly easier path away from a learning opportunity. At that young age, my wife and I naively concluded that it would be better to run away from life's challenges and try to obtain comfort with something or someone new. We were in emotional pain and our reaction was to seek comfort elsewhere. Detachment from reality seemed a good direction to ease the pain. Compulsive acts and drugs were also used by both of us as a means of escape. These escapes offered a brief respite but only succeeded in prolonging our healing. Our chosen actions as we sought greener grass, backfired and what actually happened was our weak internal value systems were further challenged, therefore taking us through additional self created emotional pain. The result was we felt less about ourselves and internal negativity was heightened. If you try to circumvent a life lesson by running from it, it will follow you. I guarantee it! It may not arise tomorrow, it may not arise with the same people, but if you don't grow internally from what was offered to you, a similar situation will eventually arise to offer you another opportunity to make the same healing changes. When emotional unrest is ignored or buried, it will haunt you in several possible ways. One might develop neurosis. Or this unrest can eat away at you as you age and surface as a physical disease (dis-ease or not at ease). The diseases one experiences are quite often actually manifestations brought about by the unwillingness to accept, forgive or heal emotional pain. Emotion is energy in motion. The ignored emotional pain might surface as an action aimed at another. If you experience any emotional unrest such as anger or blame and unload your unrest and frustration at another, it is a sure sign that you have an internal issue to heal. These are signs you can watch for that will offer opportunities to be introspective and honest with yourself. The emotional pain can be identified and healed with the actions of acceptance and treatment with a wash of love.

It is the personal disappointments, failures and challenges that build energy, which in turn can offer freedoms, inner growth and increased positive thought that takes you closer to finishing the list on your metaphorical birth clipboard. The personal falls, failures, defeats, disappointments, heartbreaks, when endured and learned from are what produces the forward momentum to take a step up on life's ladder. Doing so, allows you to dust off the dirt on your knees and continue. To help with these challenges, you can also ask the forces that be to help you realize why you are internally suffering. This process is often called prayer. Help will be offered in the form of dreams, thoughts, or situations to make known your next possible choices. It will help you to make those choices wisely and from an open loving heart.

As I grew older my mind offered me angry fears and moments of shedding what was not in my best interest, to finally discover how true the psychic's prediction really was. Everyday, I continued my lack of self-love, insecurities, victim consciousness, fear of failure and shyness around women until I found the pain of everyday existence too difficult to bear.

I have always had an insatiable desire to know more about the mind. I began reading books about the powers of thought and studied whatever entered my path. Early reading gave me some answers but didn't heal my emotional pain. As suicidal thoughts crossed my mind around the age of twenty nine, I wondered if anyone really cared for me. The mental anguish and emotional pain finally drove me to decide that I was ready talk to someone about my conflicts. As I did, one by one, I found options and subsequent freedoms for my inner fears and negative thoughts. Those inner thoughts were ego-based (the false-self), pain loving, victim thoughts, which arose from my upbringing and situations I created in my life. Uncomfortable situations arose, that I had manifested, which confirmed the makeup of my inner being. Whether my thoughts were conscious or not, those thoughts were there.

I have found that what we call subconscious thought is closer than we think. When one gets the courage to take a deeper look by using self-introspection, one can become more aware of those subconscious thoughts and inner change becomes an easier task. As I accepted my inner makeup, chose optional more loving thoughts, walked through my fears, allowed the suppressed emotions to be expressed and released, new vibrational energies emerged. The new less negative thoughts I was entertaining allowed my world to be reflected back to me in more positive, successful ways. I became addicted to challenging my negativity and have never stopped growing my self-love, self-confidence and approval of self. After the turmoil we created started to settle, Carol and I continued our marriage. We vowed to work and grow together and were introduced to a school, which taught metaphysics. It was while attending that school that I learned to say yes to what entered my awareness, simultaneously becoming a sponge for anything that could offer a better outlook on life. Metaphysical lesson number one was an introduction to the powerful universal law of believing and knowing. With the use of that first law, I began to see external changes around me. I dedicated 8 months of my life to the practice of daily disciplines and began the process of honing my mental skills. By doing so I was proving to myself that the contents of my thoughts could alter my reality, take me closer to inner peace, offer more happiness and most importantly allow me to take a step closer to

Source.

While my wife and I studied metaphysics and honed our mental disciplines, one occurrence, which offered us proof of our skills, took place. We were to attend a year end company party, held by Carol's employer. At this party, there were televisions among other items to be raffled away. In need of a new television my wife and I used our newly found mental awareness and together did our mental exercises to manifest a television. Up to that point in time, we had rarely won any contests or raffles but the day of the company holiday party, we won 5 televisions and a few other things as well. So others might have a chance and feeling a little guilty, we gave some of the items back. At that moment we had proved to ourselves that thoughts are things and became more careful of the contents of our minds.

We decided that we would begin our manifestations with a little saying that went like this, "for the greatest good of all concerned." By preceding our manifestation thoughts with this saying, we were in harmony with the powers that be. Manipulation was not what we intended to do.

Positive changes within my mind allowed new higher levels of confidence and a growth of inner peace within my consciousness. I had found that the new me and what I was witness to, were nothing more than what I had manifested due to the contents of my thoughts.

Without thoughts geared toward inner exploration one is a helpless ping pong ball on the sea of life, created by those thoughts. You might ask, what am I talking about? I had nothing to do with what I saw on the news last night. Let me inform you that if you are affected by something that comes into your frame of reference, the item you noticed is offering you the opportunity to resolve something that is within yourself. It entered your frame of reference due to your thoughts and inner makeup. I was releasing the need to react to life in a negative way by dropping the anger, blame and judgmental mindset. I began to see the options for resolving the need to react to what showed up in my life in a non-loving way. Some of these changes came quick and offered revelations, while others have been unfolding for decades. My learning opportunities are an ongoing happening and never truly stop. These options for change are present for all of us. By dedicating a life to positive change, each of us can begin to heal ourselves, the world and help man's next step toward a more positive evolution.

I can look back on my life and see the many seemingly good and or bad things I had to go through to come closer to being at peace with my main mission. Good and bad don't really exist, that's why I use the word seemingly. It's all good, once we understand the process. In retrospect I can now say that the moment I finally made the decision to seek guidance, by going to talk with a therapist was the turning point to begin my next incarnation. I currently feel like I am experiencing my fourth incarnation all within this one lifetime. I have the same name but I am not the same being I was when my life began.

It is when we decide we can no longer endure the evolutionary process or determine we have no more to accomplish, that we decide to cross over (physical death) back to where we started. After a brief rest, it is on the other side that we determine how successful we were at checking off items on our clipboard. As spirit, our soul once again realizes we are part of the Force and decisions are made as to whether we have to either give it another go (born again into the physical), or become a helper/guide to those that decide it's time to incarnate again. Another reminder is worthy of mentioning again. You do not have to believe in reincarnation or God to walk away with helpful tools for a better life, after reading this manual. If you get one new great tool, it will be worth the time and effort to continue reading. Don't let old beliefs hold you back or give reason to halt your possible discoveries.

I wish you all the luck in the world that you come to peace with this process and complete your life's mission. I sincerely hope the words that follow might help sort out the decisions you will make, during your time here on Earth. I wish you all the success possible to bring you closer to making the contents of your clipboard disappear and to become aware of your magnificence. Inner peace truly is a worthy goal. Remember life doesn't have to be as difficult as we sometimes make it. Drop the fears and let in the love.

⋄Chapter Two☙

What and Why of Spirituality

The definition of spiritualism and spirituality through the years has evolved with the times and coincides with the growth of human consciousness. Spirituality is not religion but rather was blossomed from the deemed common and most revered concepts found in all religions. Metaphysical background, human experiences and people wanting more than religion was offering, also spawned a need for what has become the modern day spiritual movement.

A spiritual journey often begins as one attempts to answer the "What is the meaning of life?" question. Another reason would be to seek answers into the absence of the true rapture and personal happiness that many humans deal with. A spiritual quest might include a search for feeling good, an increase in self-value, seeking to come to terms with death, an answer to whether God exists, an acceptance of circumstance as an opportunity for the unfolding of life's lessons, or answers to why seemingly good and atrocious occurrences happen. Michael Beckwith has said that "Religion is for those who don't want to go to hell and spirituality is for those who have already been there."

A spiritual journey often includes the discovery that everything is Source energy emanating from a higher power and discovering that you are part of that Source energy. For some, it can be a quest for inner peace, which often uncovers the concepts of being one with all, reincarnation and the fact that one is not alone after the discovery of spiritual guides. These concepts and more are provable on an individual basis, contrary to being adopted from someone's belief system. They become truths by introspection, observing personal experience and through science, as one educates himself with the current conclusions found in the relatively new field of quantum physics. Mental freedoms and a lowering of one's fear levels are a direct result of this spiritual exploration. Fear levels are also lowered with an acknowledgment of Source and a trust in its divine power. When we try to control everything in our life we tend to make our existence too complicated. When we control, we are in effect saying with our thoughts and actions that we are superior or more powerful than God. The techniques and spiritual thoughts found in this book are brought forward so you can become aware of how traits and false beliefs can stand in the way of your awakening.

Spiritualism can lead to a closer connection to Source energy and can help eliminate being manipulated by dogma (endorsing the negative emotions of shame, guilt, punishment, and concepts such as sin and obligation). Dogma often lowers the individual's ability to discover and understand one's personal power.

Spiritualism can offer higher levels of personal energy as newly discovered mental freedoms become commonplace in direct proportion to the level of separation from dogmatic control. As a result, shifts in consciousness take place and a new insatiable desire to gain additional wisdom becomes paramount.

A seeker of spiritualism begins to realize that life wasn't meant to be a struggle. Personal actions and choices start being based on the knowledge of karma, the peace discovered from

27

loving thought, humbleness, and the bliss in knowing that every person is either helping or hindering all of mankind with either positive or negative intention of thought and action. As a seeker gains a foothold into a never-ending spiritual journey along with a commitment to personal growth, he begins to experience the resultant beautiful feelings that can be generated by unconditional love, a happier life and a reduction in fear.

People who feel empty or that something is lacking in their life often want to know if there is more to life and turn to spirituality for answers. They find that to go through life only making money to be able to have a nice home and car, will always leave them empty and wanting more. There is nothing wrong with having material possessions but it is how closely you define yourself by those possessions that can become your ball and chain on your walk towards inner peace.

A Dr. Wayne Dyer quote comes to mind. "I have a suit in my closet with the pockets cut out. It's a reminder to me that I won't be taking anything with me. The last one I wear won't need any pockets." Remember that you enter this earthly incarnation with nothing and you will leave with nothing, so ask yourself what is my motivation for accumulating more? "More of what?" is often the question. A spiritual search can help prioritize and find the answers to questions such as these.

∽Chapter Three∾
Who is Spirituality for?

Spirituality is for everyone as they become ready to accept and explore the endless opportunity of possible positive change as they take steps toward understanding how they fit into the grand scheme of things. Mental search for inner peace, unconditional love, emotional balance, an increase in self-value, a healthier body, adopting a more positive thought system, having a reason to wake up in the morning, connection to Source and manifesting optional lifestyles are some of the other major reasons for becoming a seeker of spirituality.

One must be totally honest with themselves as they delve into areas of their mind that may hold conscious and subconscious thoughts that do not serve in their best interest. Many of these thoughts or adopted beliefs are not readily identifiable or exist in the subconscious area of the mind. It can be helpful to ask for help when an area of your life isn't pleasant or in your opinion, working well. David Burns wrote a book called The New Mood Therapy. I will mention him again, as I found his advice helpful in unraveling areas in my thought system that were giving me difficulty. His book is an inexpensive place to start, when one is ready to reduce the fears and choose to do some honest introspection. The key to keep the motivation strong while taking an active part in one's exploration, is in the knowing that within areas of mental awareness, subsequent mental change and by adopting alternative thought, there lies wonderful mental freedoms. Understanding the gifts these healing freedoms offer, should supersede the limiting thoughts of being flawed or wrong in some way. When exploring one's mental makeup, it is imperative to allow these positive changes to take place. In simpler terms, embracing and allowing positive change into your life is essential to further your spiritual growth or in adopting a new more

29

beneficial mental makeup. Remember, never feel less of an individual by seeking mental therapy or advice about thoughts that trouble you. Do not be frightened by mental introspection, the possible change, or thinking you might not like the person you will become. When something that doesn't serve you well is removed, a new more empowering thought will take its place. It's a law of the Universe that makes this true! The rewards are greater than you can imagine. Conversely, you may already possess inner peace and a happy life but still have questions. Spiritualism can offer answers to a more meaningful life, depth of awareness and heartfelt reason for living. You might be totally happy in this incarnation and find that you won't need the methods of changing your mental makeup as outlined in this manual but it is wise to admit we all have some item to experience or go through as we advance our soul.

One of the major keys to remember as you begin your spiritual journey toward enlightenment is that it is not as important what experiences we attract to ourselves, as how very important it is, how we react to what happens to us. How we choose to react to life is what makes all the important difference. An example of what I am referring to is the difference between how two people in different cultures might react to the experience of the death of a friend. One person might remember the wonderful gifts his friend gave the world and decide to have a celebration in his honor. The other person might be grief stricken and experiences the difficult reactions of anguish, emptiness, sadness, depression and may be angry at the fact that his close acquaintance died. For some it is difficult to fathom that their friend will not be a part of their life anymore. How would you react to such a happening? We will all experience challenging situations in our life and we will all have a choice as to how we will react to them. Bernie Siegel tells a story about Carl Jung: when a friend would come to Jung and share good news he would say "if we stay together we can get you through this." If another would come and say "Carl, I have lost my money and I have been fired from my job," he would say "let's open a bottle of wine, something good will come of this." He knew that what we categorize as life's challenges are actually opportunities for growth.

Carl was well aware that when all seemed as there were no reason for change, that #1, you aren't growing or #2, something might happen to offer a change. Through change we are offered new insight, new possibility. When we change our negative fearful thoughts to coincide with what Jung was attempting to teach us, we can possibly end up in a much more positive mindset and are therefore open to experience the next positive step.

Many who get to a point where a challenge arises, will often say to themselves "but my parents and I have always done things this way." Taking such a stance is often identified as an ego response to being fearful of change. Know that change is inevitable and to be open to change can offer you an easier transition with whatever challenging experiences come your way. Challenges are an opportunity for change. An example of taking a positive step is brought to light (pardon the pun) with the Edison story. Thomas Edison knew that if he ran electric current through something, he could sometimes make it glow. He tried countless experiments seeking the right material. When he was asked how many times had he failed while seeking the proper material, he replied, "I have not failed at all, I have merely succeeded in eliminating thousands of items that do not work." He then proceeded to find the right material and light up the world with the invention of the light bulb!

*ᐓ*Chapter four*ᐕ*
Should I feel less about myself if
I discover I need mental therapy?

Absolutely not. Change, growth, reducing or eliminating our fears, walking towards inner peace and recognizing we are part of a Force greater than ourselves, are all reasons why we are on the Earth-plane. It is much harder and sometimes impossible to change your thought and mental makeup by yourself. The mere sharing what troubles you with another will reduce its power over you. Thoughts about the opportunities and finding freedoms rather than thinking you are flawed in any way, is a more beneficial approach, when considering asking for help.

We grow up learning from commercials, doctors, our parents and repetitive situations that when one gets hurt and has an opening in the skin such as a cut, that one applies an antibiotic and bandage over it, to allow the injury to heal. Healing these injuries are apart of our awareness. But let me ask you this, when you experience rejection, failure, ridicule, war induced trauma, physical, verbal or sexual abuse, or are singled out as an example of being a less then perfect or desirable person and your mind gets injured, who is there to heal your mind? Even a close friend might say, "Ah, just shake it off, you will be fine." But our awareness of mental trauma is still in its infancy. As humans we often don't give the mental damage full attention and as the friend suggests, one might attempt to shake it off. When the mental sore gets put away into the back area of the mind, one mentally experiences an unconscious healing of sorts and often compensatory personality traits (neurosis) develop. Neurosis can develop as an ego defense mechanism. Signposts of a neurosis can be obsessive compulsive disorder, sadness, anxiety, shame, guilt, perfectionism, procrastination, hysteria and phobias, to name a few. Many of these traits unfold to keep further mental injury and pain at bay. A sheltered and less then full life is entered into and the metamorphosis of the new you emerge. This new you often does not consist of traits that motivate speedy, positive results.

Many, unfortunately still consider seeking mental help to heal from a mental injury as a weakness. It is time to change that perspective. Going to a mental therapist, life coach or psychologist for help treating a mental trauma should be free from negative stigma and be as commonplace as seeking help from a medical doctor with a physical injury.

I totally understand that it can be a difficult decision to seek a therapist, especially if your self-value system has already been challenged by your life experiences. It truly can be difficult to say once again, "I think I need assistance". But consider this an opportunity and if you are having trouble asking for help or seeking a therapist, ask yourself "why do I want to make life harder than it needs to be?" Ask "why don't I like myself enough to make things personally easier and give myself the gift of change?" Sometimes our inner voice says "but this is what I am supposed to be." When you can admit that what you currently are is keeping you from becoming what you are supposed to be or better yet, what you could be, positive growth is near. Don't be afraid of change. It is a natural process that can help you achieve a better more balanced life.

When you begin a mental introspection and seek guidance, know that you are taking a wonderful step toward making your life easier. Once you taste mental freedoms, you will want more, you will feel better about who you are and can begin the removal of the negative traits such as emotions which are associated with anger, sadness, deemed failure, procrastination, blame, guilt, insecurities and judgment. Some say, "but if I didn't express my anger, I would blow up!" They often don't realize that their inner anger is in the mind as a reaction to something and can be dealt with to release its control over your inner thoughts. A more peaceful mental place will begin to emerge from such an exploration and a dissipation of that anger you thought you required, will occur.

Finding the right therapist

A – Do an Internet search to find someone who specializes in the area of what you think you could benefit by talking about.

B - Ask a friend whom they can recommend.

C - Find support groups on the Internet with people in a similar position as yours and join their chat room.

D – Ask your doctor or a psychiatrist. Psychiatrists are medical doctors and they might be able to recommend a psychologist or therapist.

E – Ask at your church, Buddhist Temple, or place of worship.

F – Helpful therapist traits – I am of the opinion that a good therapist has been through personal mental introspection and has benefited from it. The training they go through often occurs after they helped themselves with their mental difficulty. These types of therapists are often very comfortable to be with and are passionate about helping others.

A fairly new field of mental therapy, or at least new to my experience is called Mindfulness Based Psychotherapy. This approach is often spiritually oriented but more importantly, in part, gently guides the client with relaxation self-awareness techniques and the ability to find answers from within. Mindfulness therapy can be a great adjunct for anyone, but especially for those who are ready for honest introspection and change. If you have had previous communicative connection to your subconscious and spiritual guides, mindfulness therapy may be perfect for you. One may at times think they have reached a mental pinnacle and have deemed themselves in a position that requires no further mental change. This is often referred to as denial, compensation, or the easy road to adopt. But what it often accomplishes is a perpetuation of what could be shed, which would allow the beauty that lies underneath to show its face and full potential. The denial approach is often taken from a fear based ego state of mentality, as growth is really a never-ending process. Therefore, if growth is a never-ending process one can surmise it is advantageous to keep seeking, embrace change, and continue to take steps closer to inner peace.

Walls that stop us from reaching our goals are often learned traits from our parents and early close relationships or the result of unresolved trauma. We take in most of our inner belief system and adopt what we believe by the age of 4. Other significant personality traits are absorbed by the mind by the age of 6. It is easy for one to think their internal mental makeup is a truth and unchangeable when one hardly remembers becoming who they are, due to this process taking place at such an early age. It can be difficult to get past some of these walls or even see any problem with them without help, because removing them would go against your most dominant learned beliefs. It is quite often the case that our current challenge is not the root cause for our mental anguish. The current challenge has been attracted due to the forces that be, creating an opportunity for change based on resolving a precognitive learned belief or trait. These early beliefs are part of the virtual clipboard, which was spoken of in Chapter One. Until you get guidance from a therapist or experience thorough study along with honest, deep introspection, you could stagnate and be stuck by constantly repeating your negative thoughts or actions. You might have goals that keep eluding you due to these subconscious beliefs systems. If your goals are not in alignment with your internal truths, they will be kept just out of reach. Therefore, without mental change you are often doomed to never reaching your goals. Early childhood (often precognitive) adopted beliefs or patterns can keep you from completing your desired goal, forgive another, or haunt your ego based negative thought. In my humble opinion, mental therapy is imperative to anyone who is a seeker and hasn't yet found. Think about that. It's great to be a spiritual seeker but if you have not yet reached your goal or found inner peace, ask your self this. "Is it about time I found what I am seeking?" You can read 100 self-help books, study with a guru, wear crystals around your neck and meditate for weeks but until your mind is in harmony with the life and level of peace you desire, mental therapy might just well be the action that is missing on the next step of your journey.

Personally, I came to a point where I dedicated my future to finding. I ended labeling myself a seeker and became a student of life with the ultimate goal of experiencing pure love, being grateful for all things, acceptance of what is, positive expectancy and compassion for all souls. That shift has served me well on my journey toward inner peace. If you find yourself in a painful repetitive mental position of negative thought, visualizing mental pictures of a situation that causes you anguish, continued judgment, or unable to make peace about something or someone from your past, that is a sure signal that you are in a mental bind concerning an early childhood precognitive meme or mental belief. If you find yourself in such a difficult mental place, it is in your best interest to find out about the makeup of your inner child and how to heal him or her.

One of the areas of mindfulness therapy is known as re-parenting. Many, if not all of us, were raised by parents who did the best they could with what they learned from their parents. Ancestral family traits and learned memes can often be traced back for generations. If you are troubled by thoughts that keep you out of harmony with yourself and others, for whatever reason, re-parenting can be a wonderful freeing experience. Many of us are not even aware of the learned memes that don't serve us well. We often begin our introspection based on finding out that we are not happy, feeling depressed, a lack of success, searching for inner peace, or abusing drugs and alcohol. Memes can be so engrained into your mind that we accept the fact that we have to suffer. In a case like this, we just whine, complain and hope someone will commiserate with us so we can feel a tad better before beginning another round of suffering.

There are many spiritual seekers who started their journey of awakening due to a difficult life experience. We must remember that difficult experiences have entered our earth journeys to provide a fall. A fall is needed to project you forward by the balancing needs of the energy you experienced. To get to a higher realm of energy or truly awaken on your spiritual journey it is almost always mandatory to have a fall. A fall could be a bankruptcy, a divorce, difficulty with a spouse, accident, injury, disease, loss of a job, difficult war experience, or death of a loved one. The list of what might be considered a fall, goes on and on. As mentioned before, it is not what happens to us in life but how we react to what happens to us in life that really matters. Ask yourself, have I been given an opportunity for positive change by experiencing a fall? If the answer is yes, ask yourself, "do I harbor negative thoughts about that experience? Am I experiencing strong negative emotions due to this situation?" If the answer is yes and you are not able to find peace with your opportunity (fall), therapy, especially re-parenting therapy, can offer many answers to remove that difficult burden. If you do not heal and go beyond what you needed to learn from your fall and you harbor negative inner stagnated thoughts, you will more than likely manifest a physical malady from the negativity you are bearing. Knowing this, to avoid future similar experiences, be open to what I will reveal in the next few sentences!

If you are open to change and feel you are ready to face what re-parenting might offer, pick up a copy of John Bradshaw's book titled "Homecoming". This book offers many spot on details concerning the re-parenting process. John mentions on page 63 of the paperback version of "Homecoming" that "reclaiming our childhood is painful because we must grieve our wounds. The good news is that we can do this. Grief work is the legitimate suffering we've been avoiding with our neurosis. Jung said it well: all our neurosis are substitutes for legitimate suffering." This is an important statement for when we identify our compensating neurotic actions, we can determine if we could benefit from the re-parenting process.

Old knee jerk reactions and negative thought can often be healed and eliminated by the re-parenting process. Here is an example; you are a married woman going on 8 years into the union. You find out your husband is having a sexual affair with another woman and you freak out. You are hurt, bewildered, shocked and in emotional pain about the whys and what to do. Your first reaction is to kick him out of the house and begin proceedings to get as much financial support from him during your soon to be divorce proceedings. Believe it or not this is your knee jerk reaction to his actions. Remember, it is not what

37

happens to you in life but what matters is how you react to what happens! You feel hurt, less of a person, emotionally sad, frightened that your life has taken a turn toward the unknown and you want revenge to compensate for the way you feel. You feel less of a woman, perhaps you begin to doubt not only your outward beauty but your worth as a human being. You're embarrassed and feel you will not be able to show your face to your friends, EVER again. IT HURTS! Especially in your heart and stomach area, where emotions are often centered! Here is where a personal growth can take place by actually being open to your own opportunity (fall) for change. When you search into the makeup of your precognitive beliefs (inner child) you may discover the true reasons why your husband had the affair and acted out from his painful inner beliefs and needs (inner child). You in turn might discover why you felt so bad going through the reaction to such an experience. It is often possible to not only heal your inner child by altering your belief systems but you begin to find compassion for all people, including your husband, as you begin to see that everyone is dealing with his or her inner child. A warning is needed at this juncture because re-parenting a person who has experienced severe mental or sexual abuse and is involved with addictions will find it is in their best interest to get help with this type of introspection. During the re-parenting process, strong emotions can lead to overwhelming mental situations and guidance from one who has experience with the re-parenting process will be needed before proceeding. For more information to find out where you stand concerning the re-parenting process go to John Bradshaw's book "Homecoming" and read Part 2. "Reclaiming Your Wounded Inner Child". Consult the "Introduction" which follows and continue up to Chapter 3, which begins the "Original Pain Work." The book also offers a questionnaire in the beginning to see if you might benefit from the re-parenting process.

While on the subject of parenting, here in the USA it is not widely known that it is against the law to hit, slap or spank, in any way, a child in 49 countries around the world. The movement against child abuse began in 1979 when Sweden was the first country to take physical child abuse into the political arena. Laws were past and many countries have followed positive steps forward concerning physical child abu often psychological abuse that accompanies such violent, action. In the USA corporal punishment is lawful in the home a in many schools in all of the states. State laws confirm the right of parents and teachers to inflict physical punishment on their children. Legal provisions against violence and abuse are not interpreted as prohibiting all corporal punishment in childrearing. It is of the opinion of many adults in the USA that hitting a child is in the child's best interest under the guise that children benefit from such violence. The adults that condone corporal punishment are unaware that when they justify such abuse, administered when their children do not "behave" in a manner in which the parent expects, they are attempting to make their life easier as a parent. They are uneducated in this area of parenting with disregard to the physical and psychological harm their actions inflict on the children. Abused children who have been the recipient of corporal punishment often are reserved, both physically and mentally, shy, or quiet because they have been beaten into submission and scared for life. Adult victims of physical corporal punishment and psychological abuse can develop increased aggression, antisocial behavior, masochistic tendencies and mental health problems. The next time you read about the atrocities committed where innocent people are murdered each and everyday in America stop and think about how the perpetrators of such violence developed the capacity to act in such a manner.

On the international front, physical discipline is increasingly being viewed as a violation of children's human rights. The United Nations Committee on the Rights of the Child issued a directive in 2006 calling physical punishment "legalized violence against children" that should be eliminated in all settings through "legislative, administrative, social and educational measures." 192 countries, except for the United States and Somalia failing to ratify it, have supported the treaty that established the committee. A majority of the United States population puts greater importance on money making and often support violent acts in ways that deem violence harmless or at minimum it is ignored. A few examples of such are when movies are made that are based on

39

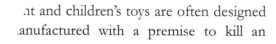

...t and children's toys are often designed
...anufactured with a premise to kill an

...on, when one enters a spiritual journey, one
...recognitive beliefs, memes, inner child, and
...that add up to what is known as the ego. The
...trolling when the needs of the wounded inner
chil... ... It can be quite a mental bind that arises due to
the interna... ...t between right and wrong, childish needs and
common sense. The ego often wins out. When you heal the inner
child or "mind" part of the mind, body and spirit, you have taken
a giant leap toward your spiritual awakening and find yourself
closer to inner peace. Once the couple in the example understood
the dynamics behind why certain things took place, they will be
able to take steps to move their lives forward in a rational,
forgiving, non-knee jerk way. Life becomes a more appreciated
journey rather than a war against personal space. Their marriage
will continue or they will enter an amiable separation. Either way
when both parties heal the internal memes, their next step forward
will be immeasurably easier.

When making efforts to balance your mind, body and
spirit, it can be extremely helpful to become familiar with the work
of Alberto Villoldo Ph.D. His book, <u>One Spirit Medicine</u> explores
the current human diet of the majority of the world and what that
diet lacks. He outlines what to do and what to eat which will aide
the body, mind, and spirit in order to allow the elimination of
unwanted brain function. His proven methods allow the body to
clear itself of toxins, and add extremely necessary probiotic strains
to the gut. These gut bacteria or healthy probiotic strains are often
lacking in the American (and other countries) digestive system and
their replacement should be a priority for anyone attempting to
achieve maximum health! Alberto's recommended diet allows the
mind to move away from what he refers to as the limbic brain.
The limbic brain is cause for many of our brain fogs and negative
thoughts. Understanding that you are what you eat becomes a
literal happening, when following Alberto's advice.

I can highly recommend Alberto's discoveries!

∽Chapter five∾

Why is it important that I become spiritual?
If the universe is infinite, can one person make a difference?

As your spiritual journey unfolds you will be exposed to many new and wonderful concepts. As you find truths in these concepts and by dropping negative traits, your energy is raised. As a result, you begin to experience a better life. As mentioned before this higher energy is your gift to the Universe and as you continue to drop the negative mindset your heightened energy level helps others on their journey. This energy increase, however small, is what you offer to all humankind, which in turn is helping to raise the level of human consciousness.

You are important, never forget that, for we are all emanating from one power and each part of the whole has the ability to raise or lower its total.

Some of these newfound concepts are more easily absorbed when viewed from a humbling perspective. Such a perspective can be touched upon when you consider how small we are in relationship to the Universe. To contemplate the infinite Universe and admitting we are but one small being made from dust, we begin to shrink our controlling ego. This type of contemplation allows us to quietly step outside our mind and look back at our situations, learning opportunities, growth potential and thoughts from that new perspective. When you are looking back at yourself from your newly discovered place of awareness, you can become closer to Source. Connecting with Source is a step towards generating honest introspection and discovering you can ask for spiritual help to generate internal positive change. You become the watcher of your life. You are no longer just the recipient of it. Then by taking an active part in your spiritual unfolding, you take a step toward guiding your life's lessons and regain your power.

Other concepts such as "we are all one" have to be proven to oneself. That is a difficult concept to adopt until we intuitively and intellectually understand that we are all energy or wave motion. All matter when broken down to its smallest known components is basically energy, wave motion or light. Once you prove that to yourself you intuitively begin to understand that we all influence each other. Our thoughts are things. We all are energy. When you influence another with your thought or action, you are simultaneously influencing yourself. We can all raise our energy by dropping limitations and adopting loving motivations into our life. As we drop the fears, we come closer to Source and vibrate at a higher frequency, or energy level. As you raise your energy you will begin to observe the synchronous attraction of new people and situations entering into your life. The opportunity will arise to prove to yourself that we are all connected and that thoughts are indeed things. The next conclusion is that it is a worthy goal to change our thoughts of fear to love and in tern, raise our energies, because we see how the dropping of our negativity has attracted a better life. It becomes clearer, as one raises his energy level, that one gives that higher energy level to everything and everyone. It truly becomes a worthy goal. To experience a wonderful YouTube that begins to show us we are all one, please watch the video by typing into your Internet browser, this link: **#1**

Some say this raising of our energy adds to the never-ending expansion of the force we call God. Adopting and proving this concept to yourself strengthens your connection to Source and will simultaneously increases your self-value system. Your self-value system is a non-narcissistic, non-ego based self-love and is one of the most important possessions you can become aware of, develop and grow.

Since the world is the creation of mass consciousness and is a world of contrasts, we can choose to love ourselves to better our experience of our world. The up side to such an accomplishment is that the resulting world becomes a better place for all.

So, to make a long story short, yes, an unequivocal yes, is the answer to the question;

<u>Do I make a difference?</u>

You already do, now choose to...
Make it an important, positive difference.

◄§Chapter Six§►

Is spiritualism for everyone?

There really is no right or wrong. The Earth-plane is a learning ground of contrasts, experiences and learning to use your free-will to make choices. Exploring spiritualism could benefit anyone, but might not be what you need to complete your purpose for your journey toward enlightenment or to complete the reason for this incarnation. Examples might be that someone has incarnated to learn how to be totally dependent on another, to release control over another or to complete an act of karma. One might be here to balance out an iniquity from a past life. Another might be here to find true inner peace and teach the world of the beauty of living in the now without judgment of another or of any circumstance. Each individual has to make a choice to determine if the exploration and application of spirituality is right for him or her at this time.

By looking within your own consciousness to determine your need of giving yourself the gift of happiness, inner peace, forgiveness, emotional balance or the power of obtaining a higher vibration by connecting with Source, you will be able to determine your current need for spirituality. While making your choice, always remember that releasing fear and choosing love is your gift to not only yourself, but to God and the entire universe. In my opinion, the opportunity for taking that step towards love is always available and there is room for such a step in each and every life.

Spiritualism can offer a removal of the fear of death, inner peace, blissful moments of connections with other dimensions and understanding for a reason for life and freedoms beyond one's current level of comprehension. Spiritualism also offers the individual cognizance of the state of human consciousness and his ability to increase that level of human consciousness.

These concepts are but a few of which can offer incentives and contribute to the determining factors when deciding if a spiritually oriented life is for you. Personally, I can see a benefit for all humans to allow spirituality into their realm of awareness. Adopting a spiritual quest was my saving grace. It brought me out of the pit of mental despair and took me by the hand to show me the way toward manifesting the life I sought. The only things, which exist between where you are and what you want to be, are your thoughts that are not in alignment with your goal.

Since my guides stepped forward and helped me take steps toward inner peace, I feel we can all have spiritual doors opened once we adopt a spiritual path. It has been said, "As we seek, so shall we find." Keep the seeker's door open! It is through an honest awareness of spirituality that mankind can shed his fears, go beyond the needs of the egos inner negative drive that most have talking in the back of their mind, and eventually allow peace to flourish in the world.

⊸Chapter Seven⊱
Where does religion fit into being spiritual and how do my thoughts affect the universe?

We are currently witness to an evolutionary swing from old-school highly dogmatic religions that were motivated by the gain of power and money into group gatherings that release the negative controls over their flocks. New church like gatherings instead of touting ruling dogma are promoting self-love, personal empowerment, empathy, meditation, inner exploration and offering a path toward inner peace. Many people now have hope that religions can evolve to serve a function for positive human development. Pope Francis has brought to light some new more accepting philosophies and shows hope that some of the antiquated Catholic dogma has room for change. Some church gatherings are now teaching how to release mental thought systems of guilt, shame, judgment of another and worthlessness. By helping to identifying these concepts, while nurturing the personal powers needed to allow their release, development of inner peace and connection to Source are often the result. It is spiritualism and connection to Source that can grow stronger in a symbiotic relationship, which will allow one to obtain freedoms and a higher purpose.

In the past many religions and churches used the threat of an afterlife of living in hell to control their members and offered the gift of everlasting life to gain power and money. Since the fear of death is one of man' s biggest fears, this fear was and is used consciously or unconsciously by organized religion to manipulate the masses.

46

When entire societies rarely talk about death such as in America, which is a by-product of a fear-based society, it isn't that difficult to gain control over the masses with the promise of everlasting life. In my humble opinion, archaic Christian religions along with some other religions have been one of the most detrimental cultural systems contributing to the slowing down of man's positive development toward a true connection to God, Source, Higher-Self or whatever you want to call it.

Man's manipulation of the truths was where the difficulty began. It has been said that Emperor Justinian in 545 A.D. was able to apply the full power of Rome to change the writings in the bible to better suit his power and position. He also used his authority to stop the belief in reincarnation by striking the biblical references to the pre existence of the soul. He forced the ruling cardinals to draft a papal decree stating that anyone who believes that souls come from God and return to God will be punished by death. **#2**

A research of how and when the Bible was written, the papal and Roman manipulation of the concept of Christianity, reincarnation, and events such as in the 12th century when Pope Innocent III decreed and condoned the murdering and subsequent elimination of tens of thousands of Cathars in France will begin to shed light on man's negative influence on religion. **#3**

A true connection to Source can eliminate a fear of death and allow one to truly open the gates toward unconditional love of self and others. This true connection to Source can be proven to the individual through experiences, which will be outlined in this manual. Once you obtain this "proof" your consciousness has created a personal truth. Truths begin to offer freedoms and fear begins to dissipate. These truths, as they supersede old adopted beliefs, become the catalyst which will offer gifts of acceptance of what is, self-love and an allowing of a more loving, forgiving, peaceful mindset.

It can be helpful to observe how some hypocritical religions can influence our actions. For instance, can you understand that killing another in the name of God, is hypocritical? Many wars have been waged with such a thought behind it. Rather than judging religion or any other past

47

occurrence as evil, we begin to see how all experiences have been necessary to go from a life based on dogma, identification with a group mentality, allowing fear, to a life based on truths, inner peace, and love. As we become more aware and witness religious evolution, one realizes that it is the stagnated resistance to change originating from fear-based ideology that slows and prevents one from positive growth. Accept that all things are in a constant state of flux, it can be no other way. Adopt a willful personal change toward love and it will help make positive changes for all. Ask yourself if that hour spent attending a religious service has lowered your fear of death and given you a boost to get through the week as you go about your life as you always have. Or have you truly been internally changed for the better? If you haven't been internally changed, you may want to ask yourself if you have accepted the offered manipulation and become complacent in your individual search for truth. Conversely, have you truly adopted positive self-loving personal change and carry it with you all week after attending your chosen church service? These are questions to ask yourself while contemplating this chapter's title.

Science and spirituality both agree that change is inevitable and both are beginning to embrace rather than resist this realization. A personal willingness to change is therefore in-line with your positive evolution. Remember that as you resist, so shall it persist. When Jesus said turn the other cheek, he was saying that when you resist, retaliate, or fight anything that you deem a threat, you will only strengthen what you are attempting to eliminate. True progression only occurs with personal change by eliminating the fear based thought and embracing the loving alternative.

Once again, as a reminder, love is the most powerful force we know. Awareness of personal resistance as one observes an internal rebuttal about such statements about the power of love, is essential in identifying an internal resistance to change. It bears repeating that as you resist, so shall it persist. That catch 22 will be the subject of further exploration later in this manual and will offer food for thought that there exists a way to evolve beyond the current state of human consciousness.

As stated before, past religious hypocrisy is evident when they teach worthwhile concepts of peacefulness and tout rules such as man shall not kill thy neighbor but turn around and condone entire wars waged in the name of God. It is an interesting concept to apply the "As you resist so shall it persist," wisdom to the concept of war. Will war persist until we humans understand this? It is a punishable act to kill someone, but condoned when you kill if you are a soldier? Are we truly acting in our best interest, by doing so? Are we removing a perceived threat? What is a threat, other than a fear? Soldiers who are taught the armed forces philosophies are used as political tools and often psychologically broken after returning from war. They often succumb to the effects and tragedies of post traumatic disorder. After committing or witnessing atrocious acts of violence upon returning home, ex-soldiers are often in severe moral conflict. Personally I have compassion for these ex-soldiers but cannot condone war. It is man's authoritarian, fearful need for superiority, need to be right, or attempting to gain power and money, that makes these wars continue. It is an old and naive comment that if all the soldiers refused to go to war, there would be no war. It's much more complicated then that but without soldiers, I always picture heads of state arm wrestling to see who will win a political or religious disagreement. It was Abraham Lincoln who said these wise words, "if you want to conquer your enemies, make them your friends." As we look back on the recent unjust wars that America has entered into, we begin to see how the citizens were duped into giving up their life by adopting the blind patriotism that can often manipulate our young people. They sacrifice much, possibly be maimed or killed in the name of preserving freedom, when in fact imbalanced political leaders often used them for their gain.

Ask yourself this, did Jesus say, "Thou shall not kill, unless someone is a threat to you and are really, really bad people"?

We have recently been witness to the beginning of another religious upheaval in the Catholic Church, as Pope Benedict resigns, anticipating the public report of Vatican wrong doings. These and many other mind-opening historical occurrences can help make one realize how often we have been controlled through our fears. Please note that all rules, dogma, man-made

49

interpretations and every law that you follow or subscribe to, whether it's a religious or secular law, has come about because one person (or group of people) was trying to get somebody else to do something which would make that one person or group feel better and lower their thoughts of fear. It is also in our best interest to realize each and every one of us is important and to never place the teachings and power of any other person over our own intuitive connection to Source.

Laws have been created to make people feel safer. A desire to reduce one's level of fear within the mind, allows these laws to exist. Most people blindly follow these laws and rules because of being fined or punished in some way. Many are fear based in their beliefs. If the majority had a true connection to Source and did not fear death, many laws that involve man manipulating man would become unnecessary.

Because most are not aware their thought system has attracted all life's situations to themselves, they lose power. Being responsible for your situation is a benefit to your spiritual growth. A spiritual person won't feel the need to be as controlled or protected by rules from without. More about how the contents of our minds create our reality will be further discussed in Chapter 19.

In conclusion I feel that each and every one of us needs to make his or her own choice to attend the religious service of choice, and understand such a choice is not the only religious path to Source or everlasting life. It is also paramount to realize the importance and similarities of all religions and to stop judging another's faith as wrong or dangerous, just because it is different from your choice. It can also be helpful to simultaneously adopt a spiritual path of personal, internal, positive change, and true connection to Source.

❧Chapter Eight❧
If I explore my spiritual side, can I still be religious?

Absolutely. Many aspects of the world's religions provide positive growth opportunities and encourage the importance of each individual. Many religions can be a stepping-stone to a spiritual life where one proves to himself that he is part of the God Force. Just take a look at what Joel Osteen has created by preaching about love, self-love and positivity. **#4**

Although it appears that some of Joel's answers are based from a judgmental standpoint and he sometimes expounds views that resonate in fear-based ideology, he has become extremely popular due to his groundbreaking reluctance to preach original sin and scripture.

There exist learned spiritual leaders who admit that the bible for instance, is the word of man, inspired by God. The Bible may not be a fully historically accurate description of Jesus, but there are many inspiring stories and words in it that if taken to heart can alter one's life for the better. It is the people that take the Bible literally or interpret the bible's contents to suit there negativity, whose lives are full of fears. Many of which lash out in a non-Christian like manner at anyone who challenges their beliefs. Remember that a belief is a thought, concept or ideology that you have chosen to believe. **#5** A belief is somewhat like "A note

51

pinned to your sleeve by your mommy" as Dr. Wayne Dyer explains it. Truths on the other hand are discovered within, they are never found by adopting someone else's philosophy. Considering that most people adopt their religion from either their geographic location or from the people who are involved in their upbringing, one can use that realization to further question their belief systems.

All religion is based on the teachings of highly advanced spiritual beings and there are many similarities that run through them all. It is only with a confident, open, loving heart that one can accept his religion as not the only true or correct religion and remain open to change. Preaching religious exclusivity is a type of action generated by a weak mind, lacking in self-love, soaked in judgmental thoughts and often steeped in a deep fear of death.

Spirituality is a 100% of the time endeavor, which guides you at every moment of your life to better yourself, remove any negative thought patterns and seek inner peace for all. Immersed in a spiritual life and connection to Source allows you to discover inner truths. These truths will eliminate the fear of death and allow you to rise above the negative manipulation from any rigid, church doctrine. Use religion and the wisdom of Jesus, Buddha, Allah, or whomever, as a guide to find your eventual spiritual growth and not as a substitute for hypocritical actions when not attending a church service.

⋞Chapter nine⋟
What does "We are all one" mean?

Energy is everywhere. The Tao or Source is everywhere. God is part of that energy, so we can surmise that Source Energy must be in all things and in each and every one of us. Everything is comprised of wave motion. Science now understands that on a subatomic scale all that is, is virtually made of energy. The currently immeasurable soul is the only spark of difference. Think about it, a rock, your body, the paper this book is written on or the computer you are seeing these words on, all consist of wave motion, energy or you could say, light.

When you realize we are all made from the same energy, it's easier to rise above ego created judgment, emotion and fear. You begin to see that the Earth-plane, in its entirety, is a learning ground for divine spirit to grow. Since we are all spirit, we are all one. That is a hard pill for some to swallow for they see the seemingly good and evil people side by side and do not want to consider they are one with the energy of another.

You don't have to condone the actions of another, but seeing that we are all birthed from one spirit or energy, connection to Source can be a revelation that frees your soul to concentrate on your own spiritual growth. Dr. Wayne Dyer would say, "Become independent of the good opinion of others." **#6**

Ashes to ashes, dust to dust takes on a different meaning when we realize that our body is made from thoughts and particles of everything that has gone before.

Our thoughts are energy and each thought influences

53

everything around that thought. We can therefore conclude that when we shift our mental and physical selves, while simultaneously thinking only peaceful loving thoughts, we are no longer adding to the unrest of the Earth.

Elizabeth Lesser says "Be a Bozo on the bus". She explains in her book <u>Broken Open</u> about how to not think that others are perfect, more successful, problem-less and without secrets or difficulties. We are all working on something. Our souls have incarned on Earth to go beyond limitation, fear and negative beliefs that were learned or adopted as a child. These are our souls goals or food for our spirit's school, so to speak. Elizabeth encourages us all to get on that bus of Bozos and tells us we are all more alike than unalike. We all share the same human foibles. And yet we try to hide our "Bozo" qualities from each other. We don't want people to think we have weakness, weirdness or worries. What a waste of energy that is! She urges everyone to come out of hiding and share their genuine self, the best self and show your "Bozo" self, as it opens doors for others to share along with you. Dropping the game of pretending everything is OK, makes each and every one of us realize we have similar connections. Realizing we are all working on our spiritual growth is also a stepping-stone to understanding the concept of "we are all one." When we see clearly that everyone, regardless of fame, fortune, age, brains or beauty is a "Bozo" on the bus of life, we make true connections with others, become less judgmental, more vulnerable and more forgiving. We find ourselves among friends we never thought we could have.

Scientists have seen how the smallest particle known to man (the quark) reacts differently when observed by different scientists. #7

The quark actually acts out the theory of the observer. The conclusion from such an occurrence is that the quark is responding to the thoughts and expectations of the theorist who is observing them. The quarks are so small that they are being manipulated by thought.

Thoughts are things, thoughts beget manifestation, choose your thoughts wisely! That reminds me of a John Lennon Beatles lyric, "All You Need Is Love" Pondering that, on an internal level, when approaching your current perceived difficulty; can be very comforting. When you go through the process of changing a negative situation or thought to be healed with the power of love, be observant of any changes in your body, your mind, or your surroundings. Is there less discomfort? This can happen when a true loving healing takes place.

Watch for such occurrences and use your observation as proof to help change your belief system. Yes, thoughts are things! When fear is changed to love, we have truly given birth to a positive energy, inspiration, and gift to the world. This gift is for all of the Earth's inhabitants, which will never dissipate.

⋞Chapter Ten⋟
How can I familiarize myself with spirituality?

Finding a group of people who seek inner peace and joining in their conversations can open many helpful sources of information about your quest. As you meet people, begin to fine tune your intuition and ask yourself or others, questions that seem relevant to you. You see, when you become the creator of questions that challenge your thoughts, you take a huge step toward all knowing. You become the observer of the contents of your mind and actions and can now select optional more loving thoughts and reactions. Opening up to spirituality can occur when attending a Unity or similar non-denominational church service. While there, look at their seminars and bookstore offerings. Study meditation: Teach your mind to be quiet so you can listen, begin to find new energy and insights in the stillness. Your true wisdom lies underneath the constant barrage of controlling ego-based everyday thoughts, and meditation can allow this wisdom to come forth. When you access this wisdom, thank the energies that exist for the communication and more of the same will begin to enter your scope of reality.

We all come into this world as clean slates ready to expand the perfect loving souls that we are. It is the learned false perceptions from those around us that begin to cover up our ability to access our perfect peacefulness and worthiness. As you get older, those learned perceptions are now perceived as our opinions (memes), we absorb filters and we choose our limitations. Beliefs become guidelines for perceived truths that we adopt for the rest of our lives. These so-called personal truths are different

56

for all of us. We base and create our reality around these beliefs. We can become so ingrained with these personal perceptions that they become dominant personality traits. They are who we become. Some of these traits are perceived as good traits. They can help us as we walk through life while others are so hurtful and difficult to adopt, we compartmentalize those thoughts and bury them in the recesses of our minds. It is the contents of these buried boxes that smolder and rot in those recesses of ones mind that will cause emotional and physical difficulties in the future.

An example of a perceived truth is a belief that one must retaliate if challenged or attacked. When in reality as you resist, so shall it persist. Resistance brings back the same lesson over and over. Think about why war and all it's unbelievable atrocity is still part of our human evolution. We are in resistance mode when we are at war. Is that enough reason to question war's validity or at minimum question why war still exists? These beliefs can make us commit acts we would have never conceived, had we not been taught these limitations from birth. It is our first and most important task to seek help to uncover and heal these limiting emotional traits. They are difficult to chase away without healing them by identification, release, observation, plus walking through and beyond them.

As you get to the point where you use free-will to release the less than healthy thought, you create a vacuum in the mind. A vacuum has to be filled with new. This is true of all things in nature. Here is an example. What happens when you open a can of coffee for instance? You hear air rushing into the can due to the vacuum or lack or air inside the can. It is a law of nature; this vacuum has to be filled with new air. This holds true with the contents of our home and our mind, as well. When you access a thought that doesn't endorse your road to inner peace, you can locate it, examine it, heal it, release it and that space will now have the room for a new more freeing thought. The key for this process to take place is to be totally honest with yourself and know that there is nothing wrong with you. You merely need to open and replace some of those compartments you created in your mind. Each time you create one of these shifts in consciousness, a freedom will be discovered. You become excited to find the next

57

freedom and the layers of that onion metaphor begins to unfold for you.

When your self-value system is strong enough to take a look at what's in your mind, you can access the contents and begin your healing journey towards peace. It is when one's value system is low and dysfunctional coping mechanisms are strong, that it becomes almost impossible to identify the areas, which could benefit by replacement. Seek help with a counselor or therapist if you seem to have trouble identifying why you have any of the following traits:

A - Do you easily get irritated and create angry responses to little things?

B – Do you have a great sadness, which is sometimes overwhelming?

C – Do you have you a need to be controlling of another or possess a tendency to belittle or judge others?

D - Do you have a habit that includes incessant talking without getting to the point?

E - Do you feel fearful that you will run out of words and the person whom you are talking to might challenge your opinions?

F - Are you constantly using your cell phone, especially in the presence of other humans, whether they are strangers or worse yet in the presence of people you know?

Traits such as these reveal an act of avoidance of your current state of mind. You are quite possibly denying where you are mentally and prolonging your potential growth!

G - Are you addicted to reading material that clogs the mind with facts, which you attempt to remember and live your life by?

H - Or conversely, read many fluffy novels that you can never remember the content of?

I - Are you prone to road rage?

J - Do you feel inadequate or unintelligent when deep down you know you are not?

K - Do you often compare yourself to others with the result of feeling less then them, worthless or ashamed of

58

yourself?

L - Are you overly staunch and ready to defend your mental position (opinion) at all costs?

M - Are you using a need to acquire and brag about possessions to compensate for your inability to find connection to Source or are you compelled to own symbols of power such as a big vehicle or gun collection to compensate for this fearful feeling of lack of power?

These types of internal thought systems can be transformed when you connect to Source.

Material possessions are often used as a plea for approval, which comes forth when a connection to the all-loving Source has not yet been returned to. It is not wrong to have possessions, just recognize whether you are defining yourself by owning them. Obsessions, neurosis and or compulsions of any kind can be a warning flag, as is being overly neat or having to keep things in a certain order to avoid the feeling of ensuing chaos. A few examples of obsessions are:

N - Addictions to sex.

O - Needing to be overly skinny or on the other extreme, over weight.

P - Being overly needy, constantly seeking approval or being wanted by others.

Q - Flights of fantasy.

R - Daily self-imposed heavy exercise routines.

S - Enjoying a challenge over and over in an obsessive manner.

T - Shopping addictions (needing the feeling of acquiring something new) can be a warning.

U – Possessing OCD traits.

When anything seems out of control or when it seems an outside force is controlling you, be aware these observances are often cover-ups. Such happenings wouldn't happen if you truly loved yourself, had a true connection to Source and had arrived at a place of internal peace. Be aware that detachment can be mistaken for passion. A person prone to depression can sometimes fixate on a detailed action such as building a ship in a bottle. What may be happening is the depressed or seriously challenged person requires something to focus on to occupy the brain. Full attention to tedious tasks can be a sign of detachment. When a person is detached he is not focused on reality. Something mentally is too painful to face, so he uses all focus on a demanding task. The end result of such a task might be a plea for acceptance by silently saying "look at what I have accomplished, I am OK." The main difference between detachment and passion is that there is joy in passion. The difference in the motivating intention is key. Detachment will often have to be determined by an outside source. In other words by someone other then the detached person. The detached person does not want to be in reality, so he will not see the options until either the mental pain gets to difficult to handle or an intervention by loved ones occurs. These are only a few of the signposts that bring to light the fact that some could probably benefit from honest introspection, a need to talk to a therapist and or to seek healing, emotional balance from within.

Once an unwanted trait, thought, or seemingly painful reaction to an experience is identified, you can ask Source (pray) for help. Always know that a higher power is there to offer assistance. This assistance might come into your life as an answer in your thoughts, a dream, intuition, a sign from a happening, a new contact with something or someone. Always be observant for that synchronous answer.

Yes, we all are creators and have power but when we think we can control, heal, cure, or find answers without God's help, we are not only saying we think we are more powerful than God, but we are often simultaneously cutting off our connection to Source's offerings for guidance. Life is short and doesn't have to be a struggle, encourage a relationship with the powers that be and ask Source for help when it is needed. By doing so your journey can be accelerated, rather then wasting time while here on Earth by extending periods of fear and pain. Consult the list of titles and people at the end of this manual for your first explorations and next reading choices. Choose the first read by intuition. The contents of this material can offer clarity, motivation and purpose for beginning your spiritual journey. The New Mood Therapy by David Burns, for starters, helps with a troubled mental state.

David Burns offers simple tests in his book to determine if there are areas in your mind that could be challenged.

Immerse yourself in the writings of Stuart Wilde, Dr. Wayne Dyer, Eckhart Tolle, A Return To Love by Marianne Williamson, Deb Shapiro's book titled Your Body Speaks Your Mind, You Can Heal Your Life and How To Love Yourself by Louise Hay for metaphysical background and more topics to apply to yourself. Go to the Hay House website and watch for a title or person's work that resonates with you. Peruse a spiritual bookstore and see if you are in the slightest way, compelled to buy a certain book, books, CD, magazine or DVD. Is the cost prohibited? Find it at your local library. Curiosity to find out more about life, questioning the reason for existence and dedication to personal growth can offer a benignant understanding of the meaning of life itself!

I can recommend changing your routine to identify or weaken the egos hold on you. Getting up at dawn when you normally sleep to 8 AM will stir the ego and it will try to get you back into routine. That is just one way to challenge the ego's hold on you or at minimum make you realize it exists. A seeker can gain internal strength by taking responsibility for all areas and actions in his life. By acknowledging that all experience or emotional reaction to experience is the result of your conscious and subconscious personal thoughts, one can begin to eliminate victim consciousness. Once again, it is not what happens to you in life that matters, it's how you react to what happens to you that matters. The law of attraction brings these learning opportunities into your life's experiences based on the contents of your subconscious thought, thoughts, beliefs and inner spiritual needs to go beyond those experiences. These are opportunities to take one more step toward the all-loving Source.

One finds it increasingly difficult to blame or judge another when one takes responsibility for attracting the situation in the first place. When you arrive at knowing that the Universe is unfolding exactly as it is supposed to and understand this from a deep connection to Source rather then a mere concept or string of words, you will raise your vibrational energy. Wisdom to live life fully without judgment will begin to emerge.

Ways that help in this journey include: Changing to an alkaline diet, (Example - less meat, any white flour products, sugar & caffeine but more green leafy vegetables (see Alberto Villoldo's book in the reference section), exercising, proper essential oils use, learning to focus the mind thru mental exercise, studying how one can increase ones self-value system, and to begin focusing on being grateful for everything you have attracted, even in the smallest way.

The power of daily gratitude cannot be overstated. Spiritual teacher and contemporary thought leader, Panache Desai would be the first to agree that gratitude is likened to the vibration of love. Since the vibration of love is one of the highest vibrations we are aware of, it stands to reason that if thoughts of gratitude are similar in frequency as thoughts of love, we should become aware of the process of being grateful. As one makes a habit of looking for what to be grateful about, positive thoughts begin to dominate your mind. Happiness becomes an easier concept to adopt and more good begins to surface. Gratitude makes one's heart sing a beautiful song. Acceptance of what we attract, whom we attract and adopting a mindset or truth about being grateful for our life's lessons, becomes paramount in a journey towards inner peace.

⋖Chapter Eleven⋗

Are you closer to fear then you are aware of?

Answering the above question requires personal introspection and honesty. When you are driven by creative desires, passion, peaceful acceptance, service to others and a dream for personal betterment, you are quite possibly closer to a loving based motivation. But motivation can be difficult to determine based on what you desire. It is wise to take a look at what is behind that ball you are rolling forward. In many cases we are not aware of the forces that drive us toward our desired outcomes. A perfectionist for example often has a low internal opinion of himself and is driven by fear. Fear of failure, fear of making a mistake, or fear of having someone judge his actions. Perfection doesn't exist, is not unattainable and will wear you down if you are striving for it. If you are uncomfortable making mistakes on your way to your desires, you are most likely motivated by fear. Being uncomfortable is a red flag for you to understand you are immersed in fearful thought and it is beneficial to identify the positive more loving opposite of your current mental place. Uncomfortable can be many things. It could show up as negative yearning, unwanted emotion, anger, judgment, blame, or need for vengeance.

Mistakes are inevitable. Changing the way you perceive a deemed mistake is one of the keys to allow forward growth. It is widely known that without failures advancement of any kind is rare. Therefore what is deemed a failure, in reality is the greatest opportunity or gift for growth you have ever been given. Seeing those deemed failures as the gifts they are creates a wonderful mental freedom. Know when one fails and doesn't own or accept their action, that one has denied himself one of the greatest personal mental gifts known by all that have succeeded before him. Denial of a failure breeds fear of failure and will be the subconscious or underlying fearful thought, which will hold success just out of reach until the deemed failure is owned. Once you accept who you are and take responsibility for a deemed failure, the realization of owning that failure brings you closer to learning what doesn't work on your road to success. To fail is mandatory and should be embraced as taking another step toward your goal! It's precisely the new approach to how you think about failure, which can offer you new energy to proceed with life in a positive manner. One of the greatest attributes of failure, especially devastating failure, is that it makes one humble, makes one vulnerable to allow the weakening of personal untruths, and helps do away with unessential beliefs.

Be aware that if your self-value is low and you fail, you might suppress being responsible for what you have manifested. Such a thought system can prolong your healing concerning your failure. Blame and denial are dangerous mental arenas. It may be time to consider what you thought was a failure is actually bringing you one-step closer to your desires! Changing your thoughts about a perceived failure and knowing that the situation is only offering you an option to take a forward step toward your chosen goal is a positive shift of consciousness concerning allowance of your forward progression.

If you find yourself a procrastinator, anxious about deadlines, devastated by negative opinions about yourself from others and uncomfortable about new situations, you are likely harboring some fear based personal beliefs. Step one in adopting a motivation based on love, is to develop a true love of self which can arise when you know you are part of the God Force (Source, Force, or High Self) rather than from your accomplishments or possessions. Being open to life and being vulnerable to whatever situations come your way, while trusting in God is always a beneficial mindset.

Fear based people attempt to control or circumvent such situations thinking they are undesirable happenings, but fail to understand to be vulnerable and open to life's challenges, is to be free. Life will often provide situations, which will make you uncomfortable, it is how you are prepared for them and how you react to them that can offer you growth and strength. Say "yes" to what life brings to your doorstep.

Life's lessons exist to help you locate and release internal negative belief systems. Use free-will to decide whether it is a positive step to take part in what life brings you. It can be helpful when viewed from a questioning perspective of "how will this offer me growth potential?" But before jumping into a situation, it is possible to avoid a difficult learning by asking yourself if your actions will affect others in a negative way. If you sidestep the ego's desire to forge on and ask yourself the preceding question, you may very well be offered an easier lesson to make the internal change you are exploring. You will have to go beyond taking part in the situation, which shows up, by taking control of the egotistical desires and heal the traits within you that attracted that original learning situation in the first place. Go beyond such a limiting thought pattern by identification, acceptance, allowing them to be and then begin changing the mental attitude or meme associated with it. This will allow that situation to cease to exist in your life. Any attracted situation will at minimum diminish in direct proportion to the negative thoughts you have released. If it arises again and you have decreased the negative thoughts, which have manifested the situation, your reaction won't control you as much. Those knee jerk reactions you had been doing when confronted with that particular situation will have decreased. Consequently, new refreshing more loving learning situations, will enter your realm of existence. Attempts at avoiding a deemed "unwanted situation," will increase the severity of a future similar situation (life lessons) until you look within and either change or drop the fear based thoughts that influence your life.

An understanding that obstacles exist and will fall in front of you as you roll the metaphorical ball of life down the road is a true freedom because when they arise, you accept them or make changes from within and continue down the road. Thoughts of a lack of personal worth and pain associated with failure subside, when such an approach is adopted.

It is sage like to take a close look at the motivations that drive your life. As you go forth on your spiritual journey, remember that love is a much greater force than fear. Shifting from a life influenced by fear to a life gently moving forward based on love and trusting in the Force, is one of, if not the most important shifts you can ever make.

As challenging situations enter your life, you have three main choices or levels, as to how to deal with them. The first level is the most widely chosen and stems from a lack of awareness. It is the learning from "pain and angst" method. As you get older and in retrospect look back at the most challenging occurrences that you attracted into your life, you will see how you became a different person due to those experiences. Hopefully these experiences allowed you to become a better person. It may have taken 25 years to do so, but you can now see the positive outcome from all that self-inflicted pain you put yourself through. An example of learning from pain would be making fun of another because you lacked personal self-love. This lack of self-love can produce a desire for one to do or say hurtful things about another in order to make oneself feel more important. This act is looking for a solution to ease a deep-seated mental pain most likely brought on by a non-nurturing childhood. Such a seemingly hurtful act will often result in a retaliatory act by the person who was belittled. The person who was hurt might do something to make the perpetrator look less than good. Consequently, both parties get hurt, have been given the opportunity to heal their inner makeup, and rise above the need to do such an act in the future. This is a painful learning that could have been avoided through an increase in internal self-love. Think of any situation that results in painful reactions. Some of these are bullying, sexual affairs, cheating, slavery, robbery, murder, and hurting the earth in order to make a profit. All these and more come to fruition due to a human mental and spiritual lack. For instance in America back in the 1800's, if the plantation owners knew they could prosper by aligning with the positive loving forces that exist, they would have had no desire to use slave labor in their attempt to be abundant. Another example would be looking at what Adolph Hitler's mind was comprised of, as he decided he needed to feel better then others. He was probably so immersed in fear of not being good enough that he decided to kill everyone he thought wasn't worthy. Alice Miller writing about hateful people has this to say "constant persecution by the father turned the former child Adolf Hitler into a mass murderer with the blood of millions of people on his hands. In my later books I have repeatedly demonstrated how the political careers of mass murderers like Stalin, Saddam Hussein, Milosevic, and others were rooted in the denial of the humiliations inflicted on them in childhood." **#8**

Another example would be the gradual change or unfolding of the concept that women are equal to men. Men dominated society for so long that women in America for instance were never allowed to vote until 1920.

A spiritually oriented person who is aware of how and why situations enter their Earth-plane experience will recognize these situations as they happen. This is the second level of learning. They will choose to lower their negative knee jerk reaction for retaliation or avoidance and take a step back to observe what has happened. They will look within to see what might be in their mental makeup, which attracted the situation to them. They will identify the part of their thought system, which doesn't serve their highest interest and will see it as an opportunity to replace the identified thoughts with less judgmental more loving thoughts. A spiritual person understands the power gained by taking responsibility for everything that happens to them. Therefore blame becomes unnecessary in a spiritually oriented individual and he understands the positive gifts he gives himself by adopting a lack of judgmental thought. As this process unfolds, a spiritual person will ask Source for help. Asking the powers that be questions such as "what I am I supposed to learn from this", instead of relying on their own limited level of consciousness, is almost imperative to producing a reduction in pain and a quicker solution. One can often ask the question, then quiet the thought process and listen for the answer.

The third level of learning involves an increase in one's awareness and intuition to a point where one recognizes the learning experience before it happens. Such a person will make the positive change within and never have to go through any teaching opportunity and step beyond karma.

This level of learning is obviously the easiest to experience but is at the same time a more challenging mental state to arrive at. By familiarizing yourself with and following levels two and three, life becomes easier to manage. At this point one will also experience an increase in the speed of personal growth and spiritual progression.

To discover methods, which will increase your inner energy, consult Chapter 10. The more you can take part in increasing your energy, connecting to Source and walking toward a nonjudgmental journey toward inner peace, the easier and quicker your unfolding lessons will become. If your manifested experiences arrive to quickly and are too difficult to assimilate, you can ask (pray) for the experiences to slow down. Remember you are always attracting. By asking for help, you can influence the speed and direction of your experiences. Your inner you may even be able to sense what your next lessons are. When that is the case, watch for what you attract and heal from within. Work on dropping the fear thoughts concerning what you are expecting to experience.

⋖Chapter Twelve⋗
What is the Bible?

The Bible is a book that has many versions. These versions all differ and contain the words that men wrote down, inspired by God. They are the words of man. "Words of man" is the key phrase in that last sentence. Did you ever get a line of people together and play pass the story? That's the game where the first person in line reads a story to the second person, the second person tells the third person and so on and so on until the tenth person tells the passed down story just before the first person re-reads the original words. The last story and the original story always differ quite a bit. The same will hold true whenever man is involved. Ego, interpretation, personal gain, language barriers and many other factors come into play. To reiterate, the Bible contains the words of men, inspired by God. It is a wise man who listens to all of the interpretations of what the Bible, or any other religious and spiritual writings have to offer, then goes within to seek the truths from those words. If that inner interpretation is based on unconditional love of all that is, then that wise man understands what Buddha, Jesus and all the other enlightened humans had said, as they attempted to teach us.

◄Chapter Thirteen►
Why do people take beliefs and the Bible so literally?

Unwavering literal interpretation of anything is always caused by a chosen fear-based belief system. Again one has to consider how fear plays a part in many peoples mental makeup. Bear with me as this information is worth briefly going over once again. A person can choose to either believe, or find truths within, through an act of self-discovery. A belief is a mental band-aid or choice and is inevitably connected to our ego and coping mechanisms. This becomes evident when one person disagrees with another and tells the other person their beliefs are false. The person who has had their belief challenged becomes threatened that they might be wrong to have based their life on their chosen beliefs. The challenged person often reacts with a brief self-doubt then quickly falls back into their mental belief pattern. Their next step is to create a strong defense, retaliating toward the person who has questioned their belief. This fear-based retaliation can often be violent and has been the cause of many human deaths and wars. In dogma based religion for example, if someone blindly accepts the concept of a promise of everlasting life and someone challenges that belief, the reactions of the person who's beliefs are challenged, are often violent oppositions toward the person who challenged their belief. Their biggest fear has been challenged!

Even Christmas and it's origins are often questioned but to a devout Christian, there is usually strong opposition to writing such as this quote from the Washington Post "Thus it appears that the Christian Church chose to celebrate the birthday of its Founder on the twenty-fifth of December in order to transfer the devotion of the heathen from the Sun to him who was called the Sun of Righteousness." Valerie Strauss a Washington Post reporter wrote about the many theories concerning how Jesus' birth date was established. **#9**

Truths on the other hand, do not need such a violent defense, as they are quite real to the person who has internally discovered and proved them to be real. The Bible has been written in such a way that passages or verses can have many meanings or interpretations. Since many consider the Bible as the word of God and many people fear death and want everlasting life, they subsequently interpret and blindly follow the words in the Bible in a way that suits their beliefs. Ironically the so-called flock becomes the metaphorical group of sheep (flock) that blindly follows an interpretation of the bible or their ideology that suits their chosen beliefs. This type of interpretation endorses the aforementioned band-aid on the fear of death syndrome. It supports fear-based thought systems. Therein lies the basis for many troubles in this world, when literal Bible translation and unwavering interpretation gives further rise to follow fear-based dogma. Ego, fear-based man, will always take action with the underlying need to reduce his fear. If you feel you have to save, change or judge another person and your emotions are based in disappointment, fear, condemnation, disgust or anger, you are operating blindly from a belief. It would be in your best interest to do some introspection and learn to heal yourself from within instead of attempting to change the world around you. It was Rumi, the 13th century ancient mystic and poet who once said, "Yesterday I was clever and I wanted to change the world. Today I am wise, so I am changing myself"

Since money is security for fear-based man, he will bend whatever rules he creates to produce as large a sum of money as possible to reduce that fear. When operating from such an internal belief system, unfortunately there will never be enough money to make him stop. Until all humans understand the forces of karma and the possibility to become secure as a loving approach to manufacturing for the good of all is adopted, money will continue to reign. A recent example would be when a food company allows chemicals that are known to be harmful to humans to be used to preserve their food. The company stands to make more money if their food seems to taste better or lasts longer with the addition of these poisons. The profit-oriented company will overlook the use of harmful chemicals by justification of their actions with decisions such as "we use these chemicals in such small quantities that they won't harm anyone." Such would be the case in the recent decision to stop using the same chemicals used in the production of yoga mats in the production of mass-produced bread products. When consumers of those chemically laced bread products became aware of the fact that they had been consuming bread that contained the same chemicals used to make yoga mats, they forced the companies to stop using those chemicals. Some religious groups operate in this same way and control through fear to create money and power. Once again it's the same concept that allows huge companies to invent and produce products that will harm another human for the sake of making a profit. This is why there is fierce and blind opposition to many seemingly benign human occurrences and differences of opinions. Such is the reason behind knee jerk retaliation and terrorism toward opposing doctrine. There can be little room for accepting another human when one is operating from a fear-based thought system.

Humans come in all different packages and all have different mental makeup. Realizing this and giving space for all

72

sects of human existence is a stepping stone toward the Christ-like loving action of forgiveness and acceptance. It is often enlightening to realize that the people, who are unkind toward another, are the people who need your kindness (love) the most.

The internal acts of forgiveness and acceptance are really gifts that the wise person gives to himself. You might choose to disagree with another person's philosophy or action, but peaceful acceptance and allowing room for opposing ideology is where inner peace can take a step forward.

Peaceful thoughts can increase only through a reduction of the fear-based thought system.

Forgiveness is the path to healing your body, your mind and the Universe, as it simultaneously shifts your consciousness to a more loving place. Observe and identify your fears. You will then be in a mental place to begin healing. The realization that your thoughts have pulled to you similar energies and experiences that were generated from your thoughts allows you to see how the Earth-plane Law of Attraction functions.

At birth we separate from our higher selves and we are in a dream like existence on Earth to experience, forgive and grow. Allow love into and flow out from your heart. When you see how you were part of what you created, it is easier to accept responsibility for what you attracted into your life. The seemingly good and or bad are all one in the same. Resist the urge to blame yourself for what you attracted. Release or heal what is in the mind that brought you experiences you wanted to blame others for and give yourself the resultant gift of forgiveness, as you simultaneously give that higher vibrational thought or gift to the Universe.

When one encounters obstacles to forgiveness, experiences repeated pain from a past occurrence, or experiences frustration with the inability to forgive, it is worth the effort to consult the book, A Course In Miracles.

The Course is a year long study about accessing our true love within by teaching us how to heal ourselves through the act of forgiveness and much, much more. To get a feel for what the **Course** can accomplish, read the small book titled An Introduction to The Course in Miracles. It is the small blue book

73

of a mere 53 pages, which can truly alter your life. The **Course** offers us a picture of the ego and how it is impossible to truly forgive without the three-step process. Step one is introspection to identify the problem, step two is letting go of the problem and step three is asking Source for help. This is an oversimplification of how true forgiveness can be accomplished, so I recommend doing further A Course in Miracles study. The results can be healing, often in an unfathomable way.

Cults can arise because people are told their fears will go away and they will be saved. Once again, one can be driven to kill another as long he sees himself superior to another, is given the promise of power and his fear of death is given a brief respite with that mental band aid I spoke of. An example would be how Nazi Germany arose under such concepts. This is another reason to seek inner truths instead of blind acceptance of another's dogma. Taking a quick look at how this fearful thought process can affect us in areas of non-biblical subject matter, brings us to an example of an internal value system which has not been given positive verbal reinforcement from an early age. A person who has undergone such seemingly benign upbringing could quite possibly adopt a belief system of who they are, based on their accomplishments, adopted parental beliefs, or a false sense of superiority. They have substituted their inherent connection to God, by attempting to feel good about him or herself because of what they do or what they have. In other words they have to succeed and acquire objects to feel good within. They might be driven to the never attainable goal of perfectionism. An example of perfectionism is when one might put themselves under the self-induced pressure of completing four actions during the course of one day. They might successfully complete three of the actions with spectacular results and still feel compelled to accomplish the fourth. While working on the first item on the to-do list, the mindset is often focused on accomplishing the second item on the list. There may be a negative yearning involved that keeps the mind focused on the worry of not being able to attain a future goal. If they run out of time to do so, or fail at completing the fourth action, they feel as if they are a failure due to focusing on what they didn't accomplish rather than the 75% they actually did quite well at. This type of mindset will produce a never ending circle of negative thoughts about oneself and the mind will always be living in the worry of the future, due to not accepting the positive thoughts about accomplishing the first three items. Questioning the concept of perfectionism, living in the now and expecting the best will help to begin the reduction of such a negative mindset.

When one associates their internal value system or self worth on what they do, when they don't, they aren't. Think about that, instead of realizing they are part of a force greater than anything that humankind could ever conceive, they feel like a failure due to associating their value from a false set of beliefs they have chosen to run their life.

As one grows and heals by following the spiritual path of self-discovery of inner truths, one knows that true peace can only come from their connection to Source, service to others and the discovery of finding Source within. Ask yourself, do you want to be right or do you want to be at peace? Having beliefs are often, if not always, a necessary step in each and every personal journey of self-discovery. What I recommend is changing the way we go about choosing our internal make up and how we look at the most important three-letter question that ever was. That question is WHY? Blindly following beliefs without seeking wisdom and change, by the asking of ourselves that three letter word is to experience stagnation! That WHY question can serve to guide us toward stripping away thoughts that do not serve us in a positive way. The WHY question can eventually lead us to allow less thought into our mind. Plus it helps us to enjoy more living in the moment while trusting and strengthening our connection to God.

When you adopt such concepts as discussed in the last paragraph and shed some of the internal fear, the beauty of the Biblical truths can become joyous tear-shedding teachings. When one realizes that Jesus was guiding us toward love, trust, and asking us to drop the fear-based restrictions, it becomes clear that we have the opportunity to grow our compassion and allow others to take those necessary steps toward peace. It is truly a revelation to realize that the restrictions of the Earth-plane are needed, so souls can grow beyond those restrictions, as they journey toward finding their own loving truths and true inner peace.

Humans are in developmental infancy as far as human consciousness is concerned! Just look back one or two hundred years and compare the level of beliefs that were a part of everyday human thought. We haven't developed as greatly as we deem. Yes, it is true that we have indoor plumbing and can fly to another city in a matter of hours, but our level of human consciousness hasn't kept pace with our physical accomplishments and mechanical inventiveness.

It is on the enlightened path that one becomes strong enough to become humble. What do I mean by that? Just look up at the stars and realize that man estimates that there are over 100 billion Earth-like planets out there and that astronomers have discovered the largest known structure in the universe, a clump of active galactic cores that stretches 4 billion light-years from end to end. This so-called Shapley cluster is beyond everyday man's comprehension. **#10**

Have you tried to contemplate infinity? It's not an easy task! It is wise to realize where we are on the time-line of human development, as we know it, and admit that we aren't as evolved as our egos would like us to think.

As one attempts to construct a system, which defines the steps to enlightenment, one can see that thoughts within our minds start with information, we deem knowledge from that information and understandings begin to emerge. Wisdom seems to be next to last, as the stage of living in the present moment, and non-thought begins to take root. Considering these known stages of human thought development, it is wise and humbling to realize we have just begun our information age. We have entered stage ONE! Realizing this, one can conclude that our beliefs are rudimentary first steps to something bigger and better.

Whether our beliefs are literal translations of the Bible or whether we are doomed to only allow self-love through our accomplishments and acquisitions, it is wise at minimum to seek truths from within. Then question our current mental make up.

A synopsis of the 4 major stages of growth that outlines the growth of human consciousness starts with information, next is knowledge, understanding follows, then wisdom.

Remember, we are merely in the first stage,
The Information Stage.

You can see that this is true by merely taking a look around. Or better yet:

Google it! Ha!

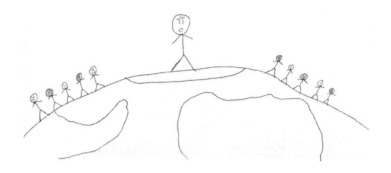

~§Chapter Fourteen§~
Are we alone?

With followers of Christianity speaking of resurrection, the fact that reincarnation was a common topic in many religions, and the countless accounts of people dying and returning to tell of their other-side experiences, how do doubts about that fact that we are not alone or part of a greater Force exist? There are arguments about whether man took all reference to reincarnation from the bible. What is important to note is the fact that there were many councils and happenings when man changed the wording in the bible to coincide with their chosen beliefs. Even religious scholars will admit that during The Council of Nicaea held in 325 AD, religious leaders took all reference to the pre existence of the soul before birth, out of the bible. Doubts concerning reincarnation and God arise from fear, lack of personal proof and a non-trusting approach to the Force. To truly

78

understand that you are not alone, I have to once again speak of seeking truths from within to prove it to yourself. When one begins to study metaphysics, pray to a Higher Power, see the importance of synchronous events and the importance of intuition, one begins to realize these are all valid reasons to delve in a little further. Synchronicity for example can be observed when you anticipate something you are deeply connected to and psychically know when that event has or will take place. Have you ever known when that package from UPS is waiting for you when you get home or when the thought of another person 2 seconds before your phone rings enters your mind to find them on the other end of the ensuing conversation? These types of events are stepping-stones to changing one's belief system as you begin to find truths that we are not alone and there is more to life then most have realized. As the bond to our belief system shifts, one begins to understand we truly are not alone and there are intelligent forces at work within and around us. What we call heaven and the positive helpers we call angels or guides are closer than you think. Connecting with the angels, fairies, Higher-Self, guides, or whatever you call that energy, gets stronger as you begin to access and trust that energies input.

You can send energy to Source, listen and trust the communication from that Source. When you do listen and trust, such as following your intuition, learning from your dreams or listening for that all knowing voice in the back of your mind, you will strengthen the connection with that loving energy. One might equate it to working out at the gym. Your spiritual muscle or link, if you will, becomes more open to you in direct proportion to the acknowledgment and gratefulness you give back to it. At this point in time, when I am sincere and need input about a current growth potential or question, I will ask (pray) for answers to come in my dream state. Before sleep I will tell myself I will remember my dreams (answers) as I sleep and await input. I can now tell the difference between normal dreams and input dreams from my guides. The communication from my guides often offers vivid pictures and some are beyond real. It can help, as you wake up, to rerun these vivid dreams in your mind and ask for interpretation. Your guides, intuition and subconscious will more often

79

than not, offer helpful interpretation. While waking up and still in an Alpha state of mind, communication is clearer. If you wait until your everyday awakening state of mind takes over, the interpretation and communication can become foggy and more difficult to grasp. The transfer of energy from your guardian(s) or guide becomes stronger if you learn to differentiate that communication from the constant thought feed that happens normally within our minds. As you trust and act on this input more and more, the bond to it grows. Meditation or at minimum learning to quiet the mind also helps open up that connection to Higher-Self communication. In short it often but not always takes effort to establish this link.

I have been lucky to have my loving positive guides, Angels, The Force, God, Higher-self, whatever you want to call such, close to me and around me, all my life. I didn't realize that fact until later in life but as I look back to consider the stand out memories, I can recognize their input. It wasn't until they saved my life, did I realize how very close they were and how fortunate I was. It was a moonless night, as I was driving my car down a dark country highway when a fairly loud voice formed words in my mind. These words didn't seem like a thought, it was a voice. It said "SLOW DOWN, DEER". I wasn't used to this type of communication, didn't mention it to my wife, who was in the passenger seat and just ignored it. It was seconds later when that voice entered my mind for the second time. It was much louder when it said the same words once again "SLOW DOWN, DEER!" I decided to slow down and watch the road carefully. It was then that I saw not one deer but a small herd of them slowing walking across the highway in a head to tail straight line. I was able to see them because I had slowed down long enough to arrive at this deer crossing at a later moment in time. The herd was now backlit by the headlights of another vehicle, which I would not have seen had I continued at my original speed. I was in a grateful small sweat when I turned to my wife, explained why I slowed down and what had just occurred. It wasn't until decades later, when exposed to the teachings of Doreen Virtue that I discovered that guides, Angels, etc, are always around us to help. She advises that we ask them for help with the lessons we are currently involved with, here on Earth. She further talks about the fact that they are always there to help but will not offer help on their own. Free will is our prerogative, which is the main force of our direction in life, and guides will only offer help when we ask for it. They will not interfere, unless a life-threatening situation arises, before it is our time to go! In that sentence were the words that made the hair on my arms stand up!

They won't interfere unless it is to save your life, before it is your time to go!

    I still had lessons to learn. My clipboard or reason for incarnation was not yet complete. The idea for writing this book had not yet entered my mind. My guides, due to a life threatening situation, had saved my life!

    Occurrences such as these are what has helped me over the years to reduce my worry about the never ending hate and violence that is so prevalent on earth. The part most people don't understand or give themselves credit for is the fact that they are also part of this intelligent universe and are part of this force. It is our less than great love of self, negative internal memes, sad emotions of loss, judgmental thoughts, and the inability to understand what we call death that tend to make us victims rather than celebrators of the process of Earth-plane experience. Yes, life is process. That last statement might sound coldly clinical. But when one understands we are all learning to change energetic thought of fear to the all powerful thought of love, in order to grow our soul, and in my humble opinion the God Force which we are all a part of, we come to understand we are part of something greater than the individual selfish ego. When deemed catastrophes take place it is our choice to get emotionally involved or we can offer strength and energy to help heal the affected. I am beginning to see deemed catastrophes as a balance of energy. How so you might ask? I see man's negativity and fear and see catastrophes offering an "ah ha" moment of sorts that make me think, "now I see what it takes to offer a solution to an imbalance". It often takes pain to motivate change!

    Getting back to how humans deal with death. I like to look at options that could follow after allowing the grieving process, which is different for all individuals. One can shift from the feeling of helplessness over the death of a loved one, to celebrating their time here on the Earth-plane. Celebrating the learning opportunities and the love that was shared between people can be quite cathartic. When you feel connected to Source and begin to understand such theories as God is growing from our progress, God is love, love is all-important, we are God, an inner shifts occurs. That shift begins to wash away the angst of common fearful thought systems.

Spiritual teacher, Panache Desai is very adamant to let us know that life happens for us, not to us. Each and every moment is an opportunity. It is very important to understand his approach and to watch how you react to such quotes as the Greek philosopher Epictetus's statement of "it is not important what happens to you in life, but it is all important how you react to what happens to you."

As you enter a truthful approach and adopt the shift toward trusting the forces that be, you realize your control was nothing more than a weak attempt at saying you were more important than God.

The Bible says, "Seek and yee shall find." I highly recommend becoming a seeker to allow the unraveling of the truths rather then wallowing in the sea of common victimization. Believing what the masses say is true, can often slow down your progression.

A humbling attitude can contribute to a step toward your true power. An interesting read concerning the topics in this chapter is Journey of Souls written by Michael Newton Ph.D.

Make the decision to drive your own ship and control your destiny. Being manipulated by others and negativity will fall away in direct proportion to the level you forgive all, by changing your thoughts to being generated by love and by trusting in God. At that point in time the blissful moments you will experience, will reveal that you are not alone.

◈Chapter Fifteen◈
My personal proof of other dimensions and the soul

My past experiences have given me insight into the existence of other dimensions. Many an atheist would be first to explain such occurrences on the unknown powers of the mind, but such a conclusion in my humble opinion is created due to their mindset (beliefs) being threatened. I also have concluded that if they had been the recipients of the same happenings I have witnessed, they might alter their beliefs about their chosen philosophies. I can remember at an early age of about seven, looking at my hands and realizing that I was indeed inside a human body. I didn't quite remember the alternative, but I remember questioning and accepting the fact that I was indeed contained inside a human body.

Later for some inexplicable reason, when I was in my late

20's, I was drawn to books that dealt with the powers of the mind and methods of meditation. As I look back, I was laying the groundwork for becoming a seeker. I mentioned the warning about the deer in the road and would like to tell the story about my next major communication from the other side. I had been studying metaphysics, dream interpretation, meditation and the powers of the mind when I observed that my companion in life was not following in my footsteps. I was internally aware that if Carol did not join me on a similar path or nurture her relationship to the Force that I most likely would have to move on separately.

I believe that people come together for karma and growth, not necessarily for life. If you stagnate, it's time to reassess your relationship and communicate to your partner about what you deem important. Your partner then has the option to grow with you or search for another path. Staying together as a couple may very well be what is needed in your situation, just don't let a partner slow down your growth. I firmly believe that it is in your best interest to grow, while having the opportunity, here on Earth.

The realization of my wife's different reality troubled me and I sought answers for my dilemma. My wife and I had been sporadically attending a non-denominational church and had met several like-minded individuals that became friends. The five of us gathered together one afternoon with the express purpose of asking (praying) to whatever positive source would hear our internally spoken words and questions. We laid on the floor with our heads close to the center of a circular spoke like shape and held hands with whoever was next to us. We sent energy to the person on our right and started a circle of vibration between us. This became a joined effort as we did indeed look like a wheel with spokes from a bird's eye view. We stated our positive intention for this gathering and asked for guidance and answers to the questions we were all silently going to ask ourselves. We took several deep breaths, closed our eyes, relaxed, then individually and internally began asking our questions. It didn't take long for my higher energies to answer my question. My question was concerning whether my wife was going to join me on what I considered the most important journey one can choose to begin. To me, that important journey is the beginning of a spiritual journey. It is the type of journey that would take one closer to Source, inner peace and enlightenment. Would she come along with me or would we grow apart? Once again, I heard the words; the voice was quite vivid in my mind. The answer I received was, "SHE WILL JOIN YOU - GIVE HER TIME". This communication was accompanied by the most overwhelming feeling of love I had ever experienced. My answer had been delivered with super strong unconditional love and energy from the other side! I get tears in my eyes just recalling how beautiful this 30-year-old experience was. Love washed over me. The communication and projection of that love was wonderful! By the way, my wife and I are still together, both dedicated to a spiritual journey and she has joined me to a point where she often has become one of my teachers.

Another experience occurred one evening when I was alone at home, very relaxed, void at the time of most of my usual mental fears and worries; I drifted off into an unexpected very deep, relaxed sleep. I can still picture the super vivid happenings within that sleep. I hesitate to call it a dream, as it was extremely vivid and real. One might call the experience a lucid dream. In this vivid dream or vision a smiling non-threatening man who was holding a few books under his arm told me he would show me proof of spirit and soul. I was instantly transported to a beautiful green valley. The valley seemed to have no beginning or end. In the distance I sensed entities garbed in white gowns that almost touched the ground. Several of these entities glided past me, telepathically communicating with me and I knew them as my parents, even though I didn't visually recognize them as parents from this life. They smiled as they drifted past. This experience in what I like to call the spirit world was very pleasurable but when I realized and doubted where I had been taken to, my fear made me slam back into my body with quite a start. That doubt not only slammed me back into reality but also awoke me with a very uneasy, sweaty feeling. I immediately drew a picture of what I had experienced and wrote down my feelings. I later discovered that my uneasy feeling might have been due to passing through my emotional level of mind, which I have since found exists between here and the level I had been shown. I had experienced all my

85

fears, albeit for only a brief instant, which had made me very uneasy. Thinking back I can conclude that it was worth it to have had that somewhat disconcerting experience. Several months later, I read a book about a person who experienced out of body travels and he described to a tee, exactly what I had seen on my inner journey. Was this synchronicity at work and personal reinforcement, once again? I like to think so.

Early in my quest of becoming a seeker, my wife Carol's mother Evelyn, became ill. It was a matter of months before we found out that she had terminal cancer and after a while, had to be admitted into the hospital. I remember slowly waking up one morning from a restful nights sleep. I was in an alpha state of mind somewhere between deep sleep and that first moment of opening my eyes, when a vision played on a hypothetical movie screen in front of my closed eyes. The vision was of Carol's mother rising slowly from bottom to top of my field of view. She was a vibrant, smiling, young woman, with red lipstick on. I remember sensing her telling me without moving her lips that all was well. I thought the vision was a tad more real than a normal near waking dream but didn't have the chance to talk to Carol about it until after we received a call not ten minutes after I awoke. It was Carol's sister Deborah informing us that mom had passed away about 15 minutes ago. Evelyn had known I was open to meet her communication and as she crossed over, entered heaven, went through transition, she came to let me know all was well. It was a pleasant happening and as I shared my vision, it became a source of comfort to all of us, knowing Evelyn was at peace.

Years later while attending a week long recording session by one of the worlds most respected intuitives, which later became a CD set offered as instruction on healing to other seekers, I was given another wonderful learning opportunity. The week had been long. We spent about 8 hours per day, with approximately 20 wonderful people who had flown in from around the globe to watch this recording in the making. The week of recording was completed. Strange but wonderful communication was offered by the Saint, which the intuitive was channeling. But it was somehow anti-climactic for me. It didn't seem complete, as the friendships we made over the week were coming to an end and we all would soon go our separate ways. An idea flashed into my mind that if it was appropriate, could we all close our eyes for a minute and offer thanks to the energies that had been channeled during that week? Everyone agreed, as did the intuitive, and the entire group did just that. It was a wonderful way to end the week and I felt good about bringing up that suggestion of unconditional thanks and gratitude. It wasn't quite 10 minutes later when I became aware of a strange feeling. A heightened sense of energy had begun to grow within my body. I can only explain it as a higher vibration or increase of energy that I was not accustomed to. I had to begin controlling my hands and arms, which were beginning to shake. I started talking to the others as we were departing concerning how wild it was to have this newly found energy. No one else was experiencing what I was, so I stopped talking about it. As my son and I began the 90-minute drive home, I explained this feeling I was experiencing to him. He was also feeling good about the week we had been privileged to witness but didn't totally understand what I was going through. About 40 minutes into the drive, I was cut off the road by another automobile, and I became agitated by the other driver's lack of common sense. I became aggravated and judged that other driver. THAT WAS A MENTAL ACTION THAT WASN'T IN MY BEST INTEREST! Immediately after I judged that other driver, I experienced what I would compare to slowly letting the air out of a large balloon. My newly found higher vibration was leaving me like someone has just pulled the plug out of my balloon body. That seemingly simple act of judgmental blame, coupled with the angry belittling of another, robbed me of approximately 40% of my new found higher energy level. I was still on a natural high when I arrived home and couldn't stop talking about the unbelievable week I had experienced. After about 2 or 3 days of getting back to my familiar but normal thought system, my new found natural high and higher vibration had dissipated. I was completely back to the vibrational level I was accustomed too. WHAT AN OPPORTUNITY and lesson I had been witness to! I was taught how judgmental and negative thought lowers our vibrational level! One of my theories to attempt an explanation of this profound occurrence was that when I took the action of gratitude toward the energies which had

87

been channeled, that energy responded in kind and gave me the gift of a higher vibration. The Saint had given me a thank you in return. That was a wonderful experience for me and a lesson in instant karma!

Another event comes to mind as I remember my aunt's departure from Earth. She was the mother of cousin John, my age, who was like a brother to me. We grew up together living in the same house for the first 5 years of my life. When my family moved, it wasn't very far away. As a matter of fact, I could see John's house from our new home's attic window. The night John's mother, Aunt Lydia passed, I was fast sleep, about 3 AM, when I awoke from an overpowering smell of flowers. I remember that strong smell, as it was almost strong enough to inhibit my breathing. I opened my eyes but the smell was instantly gone. No flowers, nothing out of the ordinary, was in the room with me. I thought of Auntie and closed my eyes. Something made me think this question, "If this is Aunt Lydia, I will empty my mind and listen to what you might have to say." I listened within my mind for an answer. The answer came immediately but was more of a quiet background thought then the loud voice I had heard within my mind in the past. I mentally heard, "there is money in the pantry and tell Johnny to stop drinking, so much"! A few days later at Auntie's funeral I decided to move to a closer seat up front. I wanted time alone to listen to the reverend's eulogy. For some reason my cousin Kira came and sat near me. The exact smell of the flowers that woke me up several nights before entered my nostrils. The smell made me sit up straight and question what was happening. This time it wasn't Aunt Lydia waking me up with a smell, it was Kira's perfume. A strong floral scent, pleasant, not as over powering as the night smell, but then again it was exactly the same fragrance. To this day I have a suspicion that Kira's perfume smell was given to me by my Aunt a few nights before the funeral. She new what I was going to smell at the funeral and wanted to confirm that it was indeed Aunt that told me about the money and John's love of beer. I told John what had transpired, the smell, the communication, the funeral perfume and the synchronicity. I told him about the pantry money and that his mother had recommended to him to stop drinking so much. He smiled, thanked me and never brought the story up again. I was never able to confirm whether there was money in the pantry. It was either a secret or just never spoken about, but I have to say that when John died in a drowning accident, a mere six months after his mom passed, I truly felt I had once again experienced communication from the other side. An autopsy of John's body revealed the cause of death was drowning due to intoxication.

I have experienced many other gifts of communication, intuition, clairaudience and guidance during awakened moments, dreams and meditations. Dedicating my life to eliminating negativity, limiting uncomfortable thought systems and fear along with being grateful for my helpers, has grown my closeness to the positive energies that be. For the freedoms, which were discovered, I give another big "THANK YOU".

All these occurrences and many more have given me the gift of knowing what we call death is merely a transition and has guided me toward the conclusion of not fearing death. I also have a better understanding of how my mental make-up and vibrations had attracted all the personal happenings into my life. I now take responsibility for what I experience and watch for any unwanted thought of blame, which may enter my mind. Those thoughts are opportunities to choose a thought that would be less likely to lower my vibratory (energy) state.

The soul, in my humble opinion, is your true inner essence. It is your personal part of God. This part has separated from Source for the purpose of experiencing the physical and growth opportunities. Growth always offers choices, which involve either stagnation in fear or freedoms and growth discovered through love. My soul, that piece of my higher self, which decided that some time on the earth-plane would be just what I needed to grow my energy, has entered this current physical body and allowed my soul to do just that. I have broken some of the paradigms of my ancestor's history of mental challenges and I am deeply grateful that my children won't have to endure some of the experiences I had to go through in order to break those challenges. They have been spared the experiences I had signed up for. Sure, my children are working on their own challenges. That's how we all give the gift of a higher vibration to all things,

89

including God.

The combination of all souls growth and subsequent raising of human consciousness may be the way the Universe expands, or gets us one step closer to eliminating separateness from God. The soul is connected by energy to all things and each and every one of us has a unique one. Energy is energy and it exists everywhere. Our souls have the privilege of being aware of that energy and how that energy connects with all things and all beings. We are all one with God and subsequently with each other.

What is God? You might ask. We all have an idea about such a question. I might interject that we are but one grain of sand in an infinite reality. How then can we truly define God? It's just not possible. Infinity and God's magnanimous qualities are impossible for our limited minds to grasp. As far as I am concerned, God could have siblings. They could be creators of other Universes. Our God is the source of all we are familiar with and the level of love our God exudes is most probably beyond our comprehension. I have felt some of that love. It was amazing! But let's get back to that siblings theory. God's sibling might be the creator of another Universe. An experimental Universe based on fear instead of love, as ours is. If such a happening were true, then we better start basing all of our thoughts, intensions, and actions based on love instead of fear. Why? Because if the fear based Universe wins out the experiment, love might lose! I have to support the Universe based on love!

All of what is, as we know it, is depending on it!

Please e-mail your spiritual experience story!
I will listen.
aquarianspiritualdiet@gmail.com

Watch for updates, new spiritual ideas, Buddhist and
spiritually humorous Tee Shirts @
www.newspiritualitydiet.com

❧Chapter Sixteen❧
What is the most useful application
we can derive from astronomy?

When Carl Sagan said something like this, "The most useful application of astronomy is the deflation of man's most common conceits," he was reminding all humans to stay humble, become open to going beyond our internal makeup and learn to grow and change. As I have mentioned before, never underestimate the value in being humble. The vastness and infinite qualities of space will make you humble as you attempt to see your soul's place amongst its vastness.

We live on a small, pale blue spec of dirt and water in a galaxy that contains billions of stars. Our galaxy is but one of billions of galaxies that exist in a universe which is expanding into infinite space. How well can you grasp that concept and does it make your ego's self-centered thoughts dwindle in importance? It should.

We are so infinitesimally small and the study of the infinite Universe's vastness reminds you to keep the ego at bay. The ego makes us the center of the Universe, and it may help your spiritual journey to switch such a thought 180 degrees while remaining humble. Remaining in awe of our place in the Universe also helps one to become compassionate about each other and is a reminder to treat our beloved, patient, Mother Earth, with the respect she deserves.

When the ego is at bay, you begin to access your connections to Source.

Your contemplation of astronomy can help to allow that connection, to happen.

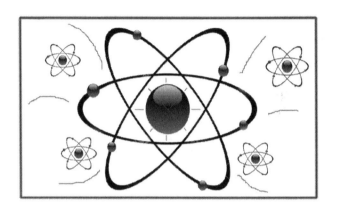

◦§Chapter Seventeen§◦
How has science started to conclude
that we are all energy?

Have you had the curiosity to watch the film called <u>What the Bleep Do We Know?</u> This movie attempts to dip your feet into the topic of Quantum physics. Quantum physics explores the micro makeup of matter.

    Descartes and Newton surmised that the physical realm existed by a set of rules that applied to all matter, rules that could not be swayed. Einstein challenged those rules with his theories that proved matter was physical but also energy or wave motion. He witnessed light for instance was energy and particles, which behaved as both when exposed to different stimulus. On a subatomic level we now can witness the components of an atom and have discovered the atom is not solid but is composed of more empty space then matter. This empty space is energy or frequency patterns of information. Everything is made of more of this energy than matter and we now can conclude there is little or no solid. If what we used to consider solid is not solid, then matter might better respond to Einstein's equations. The atom as far as the experts in the field of Quantum physics conclude, is 99.99999% energy and .00001% matter and an electron cloud surrounds the physical nucleus. Knowing that nothing is solid, on an atomic level we also see atoms reacting to different sets of rules. This excerpt from Joe Dispenza's book called <u>Breaking The Habit of Being Yourself</u> attempts to explain this phenomenon. "At the level of electrons, scientists can measure energies dependent characteristics such as wavelength, voltage potentials and the like, but these particles have a mass so infinitesimally small and exist so temporary to be almost non existent. This is what makes the subatomic world so unique. It possesses not just physical qualities but also energetic qualities. In truth, matter on a subatomic level exists as a momentary phenomenon. It's so elusive that it constantly appears and disappears, appearing in three dimensions-in time and space-and disappearing into nothing-into the Quantum field, in no space, no time-transforming from particle (matter) to wave (energy), and vice verse."

Further experiments found that this energy and matter responded to mindful attention. In other words they behaved as the experimenter thought they would behave. The parallelism here is that each experimenter proved his theory to be correct because the energy behaved different based on the experimenters thoughts about how they should behave. Thought had changed what we call reality. Contemplate the possibilities of what that last sentence implies. I suggest you do further study of Quantum physics to get a better fix on the importance of how your thoughts create what you experience. Quantum physics can further explain how the frequency or vibrational energy of your being determines what you are witness to.

Chapter Eighteen
What do these scientific studies about energy
have to do with me being spiritual?

Since everything is mostly energy and a little matter, we can begin to theorize that thought is energy. Therefore we can begin to understand thought truly can affect things. One of the most important discoveries concerning the study of Quantum physics is how matter responds to thought. Once we learn these facts about energy and matter using a left brained analytical perspective, it becomes easier to allow right brained based experiments. Small tests or experiments with the power of our thought becomes a game of changing the stop light from red to green, moving a cloud, or visualizing and manifesting the parking space you wanted. At the point of discovering truth with such experiments one needs to take a step to the side and realize the powerful implications of what he has just proven to himself.

When these experiments are taken seriously one looks back at his mind, his thoughts, his power as a creator, and takes responsibility not only for what he has created but begins to wisely choose his current thoughts. At this juncture, it becomes logical to challenge what his mind (thought) is made of and identify the ones based on emotional imbalance and fear or the ones based on love. After indentifying the negative fear based thought and a conscious positive loving shift begins to take place, the benefits of doing so are discovered. As each individual learns how to shift fear-based thought to thought based from a loving perspective,

95

human consciousness is raised.

All of your thoughts are creating your future. Don't worry about the content of your past thoughts, be concerned with changing your present thoughts to more positive loving thoughts. Your future will eventually begin to reflect those changes. The world will reflect your thoughts, as long as you are truly aligned with and have adopted these new loving thoughts, as truths.

These purposeful shifts in consciousness will initially be motivated from a selfish ego-based place but as the ego diminishes, will begin to shift from knowing the effects of karma and knowledge of how ones thoughts affect every other atom, particle, energy or person in the Universe.

These positive shifts in thought can humble a being and simultaneously begin an acceptance of true loving connections. Connections as mentioned before such as the concept that we all are created from one energy. One no longer sees himself as separate from other humans and other life forms from the humble blade of grass to the Universe itself. As these concepts get internalized one begins experiencing a lessening of fear, an increased connection to all and Source energy. Eventually this and other truths, as they emerge, take you down the path, which can eventually remove the fear of death. When the fear of death is eliminated, fear itself no longer rules one's life. There is no longer any need to profile any group or person and justify their elimination because they are different then you. The need to protect oneself with weapons is also eliminated for when one emanates only love he understands he is safe. If the Universe says it is time to die, he accepts such and knows it is only a changing of form. Nothing to fear or worry about is truly a wonderful place to experience.

❧Chapter Nineteen❧

If everything is energy, how can I prove that

thoughts are things?

Being aware of your thoughts is the first step in identifying how they affect your reality. It is recommended that you become the observer of your thoughts. You then are aware of the marvelous gift of identifying the thoughts that are not serving you and become aware of your ability to make a conscious choice to change them. The thoughts, which are usually not beneficial, are thoughts that bring you to a place of unrest, anxiety, fearfulness, self doubt, or contribute to your emotional pain such as, hate, blame, anger, judgment or self-degradation. These are thoughts that are lowering your vibrational energy and steer you away from a place of inner peace. Thoughts such as these are also reflected in the current state of your body and general health.

To begin your quest to prove that thoughts are things, start by watching for synchronous occurrences such as thinking about a person just before they call you on the phone. Or having the same thought or spoken words simultaneously with another who is in your presence. As mentioned before you can practice visualizing or seeing in your mind the parking place you want. Then watch as those spaces manifest for you. They will happen frequently based on your concentrated focus, visualization ability and lack of doubt within your belief system.

As you study about mental concentration and visualization, become aware of how your chosen physical items and wanted occurrences, which you visualized, are attracted to you. There is a very real progression you need to be aware of. As your thoughts become more focused and powerful and you begin to know and believe (find truth in) without doubt, you will gain the momentum to manifest your desires. Being aware of your intention and how your mind chooses a desire is of paramount importance. You may have a strong negative yearning to travel somewhere. You pine for seeing the Greek Islands, for instance. You are sad that you have never seen the white washed buildings of Santorini or tasted a cold glass of Greek wine by the seaside. It is what you want but seems out of reach. The deep thoughts in the back of your mind are saying, if only….. This is negative yearning, not choosing a desire. When a negative yearning is involved, your thoughts are riddled with doubt. When manifesting, it is wise to change negative yearning to positive expectation! Can you feel the energetic difference when you are able to do just that?

Please be aware of the learning opportunities that can enter your realm of experience before your desire is manifested. When you choose or visualize a desired outcome, the forces that be are engaged. You can take concerted action, but is not your place to force the creation of the desire, allow the forces that be, to unfold it for you. Drop the need for total control and be flexible on your journey. After you choose your desire, a situation might arise that will give you the opportunity to learn about a limitation that you possess. Sometimes these situations can be uncomfortable learnings based on your stubbornness or in direct proportion to how hidden they are in your mind. If you are honest with yourself and look within to identify what you need to go beyond based on this situation you attracted, you will be aware of what stands between you and the manifestation of the desire you asked for. These growth opportunities are there to allow you to use free will to shift an internal thought system from fear-based to love-based. They are also there to give you the opportunity to identify what you need to go through (never around) and learn what needs to be internally changed which could allow you to get closer to what you asked for. These learning situations allow you to grow and give you the opportunity to remove the variance that exists between your current vibratory state and the vibratory state required for you to manifest your chosen situation or that physical item you desire. Take responsibility as a creator, and nurture an attitude of manifesting for the greatest good of all concerned.

It is possible to come to a point where you will be ON the Earth- plane but not "PART" of it. You begin to separate from the Earth-plane when you realize that Earth-plane existence is a learning ground for experience. You will understand that experiences exist for the sole purpose of finding a healing path back to Source and the subsequent allowing of the growth of Source or God-Force. You will be able to allow all the happenings, which go on around you as a necessary occurrence, learn from them and concentrate on your own growth of inner peace. You can increase thoughts originating from love and begin to experience the death of thought, as we currently understand it. As you create a thought system of peace and love and eventually live in the present moment, fear falls by the wayside. This type of mental possibility is the precursor to a reduction of thought. The observer starts to lovingly live in the now, the only place in time that matters, as it is not influenced by the angstful judgmental thoughts of the past nor full of anxiety and fear of what might happen in the future. The point of power is the NOW. Peaceful thoughts create more peace in your world. To test this concept of non-thought in relation to the elimination of internal fear, become the observer of the contents of your mind. Identify when the false self or ego has taken over and you are in a painful, negative mental place. This mental negative place might be a worried mind or anger aimed at another person's past action. You might have an internal need to verify you have been the victim in a situation. When you have identified the pain you are experiencing, take a timeout and begin concentrating on your breathing process. Breathe in, breathe out, and repeat. Put your mental focus on your hands. You might be able to feel a tingle in your fingers. Allow the original negative thoughts to drift away from your mind like a small white cloud on a beautiful day. Concentrate on the breathing as you look at something in your immediate vicinity. Maybe a swaying leaf as the wind gently moves it left and right. If you can keep this alternative non-judgmental mental state in the foreground of your mind, you will at one point discover the pain from the original thought had been given a brief reprieve! What does that prove, you might ask? It proves you have a choice to think whatever you want. You have a choice to eliminate a negative thought by replacing it with a thought that will serve you well. This is always an option, which in turn, can offer you a sense of internal peace. When you realize this is possible, your goal then becomes a journey to heal that original worrisome or angry thought that arose in the first place. One can do this by introspection of the internal mindset that originally created the situation you are currently worried or angry about. Your world is always willing to change, in direct proportion to the healing from within. These are the first steps toward a choice to heal and toward an introduction into non-thought. Never attempt to bury a negative thought. As said before what you resist, shall persist. Buried negativity will eventually lower your energy and show up as a disease. This is precisely why it is mentioned in the preceding sentences that it always a better approach to heal the negativity, not cover it up.

A great freedom arises as we begin to release the need to fix the world. Through understanding and wisdom we start to understand that the Earth must be as it is, until all humankind has gone beyond the need (learning opportunity) of the situation we thought we needed to control, end or fix. There is a story about Mother Teresa that puts this into an easy to understand perspective. She was asked to march against war, and she politely refused. She then said "but if you are having a gathering to promote peace, let me know." **#11** Do you see the difference?

100

Resistance versus the choice to creative a positive state is the peaceful and powerful difference.

As we come to realize thoughts are things and do indeed create our next moment, we can choose to create a beautiful place of being. We can simultaneously eliminate negative thought and become immersed in an all-trusting loving consciousness. This blissful state of heightened awareness exists beyond the realm of what we understand thought to be. According to Eckhart Tolle, man's arrival at that place of non-thought is essential for human survival. #12

I offer the concept that as you choose thoughts that originate from a place of love, your fears will begin to dwindle. By being the watcher of the contents of your mind you would then observe the positive changes that occur in your life. These changes in your physical reality will have changed for the better due to your positive shift in consciousness. Positive changes which show up in the world around you are a reflection of your inner being and will change in direct proportion to the level of your new positive loving thought system. The observance of this concept becomes a truth as you begin to see the results of cause and effect, which has been created by your new thoughts. Thoughts are things, thoughts manifest, choose your thoughts wisely. This concept is offered as a precursor to Tolle's non-thought theory or at minimum a stepping-stone toward it.

One comes to conclude that the reactions to negative emotions, which exist in the realm of ego-based thought, might very well become the cause of man's ultimate demise. It is in the best interest of humankind to at minimum learn more about each individuals possible contribution to human evolution. As one seeks a spiritual path of honest self-discovery, becomes responsible for the contents of their mind, and by changes made toward a more loving consciousness, a rising of one's energy becomes evident. How so, you ask? Because after you learn that you can make your life better by applying the aforementioned concepts, motivation for more personal exploration, eradication of personal negativity become paramount and a life based on loving thoughts becomes a priority. This is a somewhat selfish start but is a beneficial occurrence, as it is often the first step to the "ah ha" moment of realizing that personal change can be beneficial to the world and to others. Be patient and observant. Sometimes thoughts, which shift, take more time then one expects. This is precisely why the old saying of "time will heal" was passed down in many cultures. What was missing were the facts that we can assist that healing, and that the reason that time heals is due to the fact that it is a shift in consciousness which facilitates the healing change, not the passing of time.

I remember back in the late 80's, a wise spiritual teacher was addressing us in a large group. He would run up to individuals and almost shout in their face "What Do You Want!" He was shocking us to realize many of us did not have our desires in the front of our thought process. Some of us didn't know at all. Most of us had to think about it and before we would come up with our answer, he was off to the next person, shouting at them. "What Do You Want?" Some of us would say "to be rich." To that he replied, "The Universe doesn't know what RICH is! Be specific!" He was forcing us to not only become aware of our desires, but to be specific about them as well. This leads me to another teacher who taught us to make a ten most wanted list. She said, be specific and write those ten desires down on paper at least once a day. She recommended that we refine the list as desires change or they find manifestation in our lives. Another teacher took it a step further by teaching to see those desires in our minds as they already existed. See colors, and internally experience any senses that would normally accompany those desires. See those desires as real and with emotion. For example, if it was a new convertible car you desired, know the make, see the desired color, smell the new interior and feel of the wheel as you drove around in it. Feel the wind in your face and emotional excitement of driving, while feeling gratitude for having the new vehicle. These were wise interesting teachers who were aware of how the manifestation process functions. These are some of the techniques you can use while refining your visualizations. My take on this list now that I have seen how the Universe works, is to change the "Ten Most Wanted" list to the Ten Most Expected List!"

The shift that was predicted by the theories of the Mayan 2012 apocalypse (#13) was actually a sign for the opportunity to join others in rising to the next level of human consciousness, before the either literal or symbolic annihilation of humanity takes place. A great book to start with when seeking answers about the power of your thoughts and how it influences your reality is: E-Squared: Nine Do-It-Yourself Energy Experiments That Prove Your Thoughts Create Your Reality by Pam Grout. This book includes experiments you can do to begin proving to yourself that thoughts are energies and can work for you, and is offered on Amazon.

❧Chapter Twenty❧
Healing disease and respecting the power of thought.

This quote is from the King James version of the Bible: *"And Jesus said unto them, Because of your unbelief: for verily I say unto you, If ye have faith as a grain of mustard seed, ye shall say unto this mountain, Remove hence to yonder place; and it shall remove; and nothing shall be impossible unto you."*

Please do not take your creative power lightly. Your thoughts are things. They have creative power and should be respected. Take responsibility for all your conscious and subconscious thought and the resultant manifestations of those thoughts. It is also helpful to know that there exists a greater level of manifestation power in numbers. A small group of people all on the same mission can be much more powerful than an individual. That is why it is important for you to awaken to the power of loving thoughts. Because as you do, the positive energies you emit will help increase the level of positive growth for all of humanity.

The positive and negative polarities when male and female energy come together, also helps increase the powers of

104

manifestation over the individual. The two opposite gender qualities are working together and become a singular more powerful force. As human consciousness rises male humans will accept female humans as their equal, if not spiritual superior. He will rise above the base sexual desire to take and dominate and eventually discover the full powerful potential of how selfless giving during daily routine and the act of love making, can benefit all involved. A coming together of two or more people who seek to channel divine energy for the greatest good is often called a tantric practice. Tantra can also be associated with a coming together between two people of the opposite sex in an agreed upon sacred act of lovemaking. A mutually agreed upon dedication of the powerful energies created during this act can be consciously directed before the act takes place, to further aid in the creative manifestation process. **#14**

It is a wise person that manifests with the mental undertone "for the greatest good for all concerned". That statement tells the creative powers that be that you are opting to stay off the treadmill of negative karma, for you are creating and allowing, not manipulating. Attempting to force your energies on some situation that you think needs changing or on a person that you feel badly towards is a sure fire way to produce future negative results for yourself. You will never know when the ball of balance (karma) might opt to roll over your toes. If you doubt the validity of karma there are observations you can look for in an attempt to see what is at work through the forces of balance. Look for seemingly good or seemingly bad things that happen to yourself, based on your past actions and or thought. Do these situations or things that you have unconsciously manifested, seem to make cause and effect sense? If you are honest with yourself, I deduce that you will find validity in this cause and effect observation. The same holds true for what we might call a negative occurrence. It could be as simple as killing some wasps and 24 hours later, getting stung.

Have you experienced an unwanted accident such as a fender bender with your car or something as simple as dropping a glass jar only to witness its contents spill onto the kitchen floor? If you can say "yes" to these questions, the next time you experience a similar occurrence, stop, take a deep breath and ask yourself if you are out of balance. You may be in a rush, you may be seeking perfectionism in your action, and you may be thinking a fear based thought about a future event. In any case when you are in an accident-prone place in time, slow down, shift your thoughts, take a deep breath, concentrate on the now moment in time and center yourself. You will quickly find yourself climbing out of that lower vibrational accident-prone, karma inducing mental space.

When you are free of ego, free of negative emotions, filled with loving thoughts, expect the best, are thankful and have no fear; you will not emit energies that would adversely affect yourself or another. What you experience will be deemed as not wrong, no matter what! The positivity you will exude will effect every atom, every plant, every animal, every person, everything. But conversely if you are a selfish ego-based manipulator, you will have to go through the karmic balancing effects of your intentions and actions. Remember that energy doesn't die it just changes form. One might not experience the effects of karma in this life but balance might take place in another.

Disease is actually better thought of as two words. Dis & Ease. In other words karma, dharma or a lack of ease is what causes disease. Belief systems are all powerful influences on our health. Dr. Wayne Dyer had claimed that there have been examples of families where both parents developed a particular disease. Their adopted child also acquired the same non-communicable disease. This is another possible example of how the power of similar thought, can be transferred from one person to another. The parent had transferred their emotional imbalance and fear thoughts to the child and produced the same physical outcome. If these people were from the same bloodline, most Western doctors would cite this as a hereditary issue, but it is the similar thought system that manifested the disease firstly and perpetuates the imbalance. Since thoughts are things or energy, they can be absorbed and transferred in many ways, not only from word of mouth.

Some Buddhists would say thoughts of desire and high future expectations are the cause of your suffering. Others would say a denied desire could fester within and cause disease. It should

106

be noted that a desire begins manifesting, as soon as its choice is decided upon. The only thing that stands in the way of the desire and instant manifestation is a persons thoughts that are not in harmony with the chosen desire. When a desire is chosen, the Universe will bring thoughts or situations into one's life to challenge the inner beliefs that are not in alignment with the chosen desire. The average person normally sees these seemingly uncomfortable challenges as a negative occurrence. The seeker, on the other hand, is observant of what has been attracted to their life's situation and will seek a way to identify and heal the inner uncomfortable belief or thought that stands between his current reality and the new desire he is seeking to attain. Once the internal balancing or healing of a negative belief or thought system takes place, the situations, which were attracted, will begin to fade away. New opportunities and situations will surface (be manifested) based on the contents of the mind. This is a simple explanation of how a soul journeys back to Source. When one denies the illusion of the ego and emanates only love, he is getting closer to home.

There has been research showing how buried emotions and a lack of forgiveness will eventually produce disease. Some say all disease is nothing more than a forgiveness issue. Making the decision to become happy and experiencing true forgiveness of another or of yourself, can be two of the most important acts you can personally experience when seeking the elimination of a physical or mental disease. When these decisions are truthful to self and internal changes are real, a shift in consciousness will be felt. These new feelings will be a result of your vibrational changes, for the better. All thoughts associated with the act of forgiveness need to be explored and healed. Many of these thoughts can be subconscious or have been adopted by your early belief system. Once you can identify them and completely forgive, you can expect healing to take place. Introspective research to find, heal and change a fear, meme, negative, or uncomfortable thought, will often result in healing miracles. Forgiveness is a gift you give yourself, not a pardon to the party who seemingly wronged you. You do not have to condone the action of another to forgive them, but in attempting to understand their motivation you can begin to understand the why's of the situation and how your inner make up contributed to and attracted the act in the first place.

As one finds acceptance of a past occurrence, a newfound compassion begins to grow. Secondly, a subsequent release of inner anger, need for revenge and hatred aimed at another, melts away and offers a healing gift, that most are not conscious of its possibility.

As you forgive and heal from within it is very important to assess your level of vulnerability. What do I mean by that, you ask? An example may be in order, to better bring what I mean by vulnerability, to light. Let's say that you put yourself through mental anguish over a situation that compromised your trust in another. The person didn't behave in a manner that you wanted them to behave in. Your trust was compromised and you unconsciously decided to experience hurt, anger, sadness, and began building a system of distrust. You mentally tried to protect your heart from further attack. You then begin a journey, one that included a search for inner peace. You read this or a similar manuscript and decided that it was time to give yourself the gift of forgiveness. One might encounter hurdles on the path toward true forgiveness and have difficulty getting to a peaceful conclusion without being vulnerable. Personal introspection most likely will result in a wall around the heart energy. This blockage is an energy wall that was created to protect against experiencing those painful emotions again. Here is where a personal vulnerability analysis would be beneficial. If an individual is protecting himself from further experiences by creating inner mental walls in an attempt to guard from future pain, the possibility to truly forgive or completely love becomes impossible. Removals of the self-created mental and emotional guards, therefore becoming vulnerable, are prerequisites for complete inner healing. You cannot walk around your fears you must walk through them and safely give them room to get as large as they want. Since these fears and emotions are energy, they need to be embraced to allow them to be expressed and dissipated. To expect true inner peace without becoming vulnerable is virtually impossible. Opening oneself to love, removing self-generated guards, and diving headfirst into life, makes you vulnerably ready to experience life to it's fullest.

Common man is usually seeking revenge, generating anger or victim thoughts and overlooks the possibility for a peaceful resolution. As one seeks a true connection to Source it is imperative that forgiveness replace all possible inner conflict and turmoil. Personal forgiveness plus forgiveness of others is a mandatory step to a true connection with Source in order to experience inner peace and total well being. As one gets closer to a true positive shift in consciousness, watch for any remaining negative thoughts, learning situations or new physical problems to arise. These new challenges or opportunities can often be a reaction manifested by the stubborn unwillingness to change brought on by the ego. If the ego attempts to keep you from obtaining a new higher vibration as you heal, it is in your best interest to have an inner talk with your ego and assert who is boss. It is possible to love ones ego and at the same time have an internal conversation that places it in your heart with love. After such introspection you can also tell the ego to rest because you are now driving your destiny. It's quite possible to lower the egos knee jerk negative reactions with such a loving approach toward it. It bears repeating that as you resist, so shall it persist. Apply this concept to all situations and bring love to the table as an alternative approach for resolution and positive change. As the observer of the contents of your mind, watch for negative thoughts that are associated with your healing process and continue replacing them with more loving thoughts. Tell the ego you are continuing on your loving healing journey and lovingly tell it to cease in its attempt to control your body with negative thoughts or the manifestation of a new replacement disease.

Affirmations can be another powerful place to begin changing not only your thought process but also your energy on a cellular level. For instance, when one has a low self-value system, it may be a difficult task to silently say, "I completely and totally love and accept myself". But with repetition (and I mean hundreds of times a day), the mind can begin to respond to positive affirmations just as it had responded to your negative ones. Worry for instance is a negative affirmation and fear of the future. Worry can add power to manifesting a future with exactly what you do not want. When it comes to positive affirmations, keep at it! Put emotion behind the affirmation for maximum results. It is the feeling behind the words that make affirmations and visualizations become much more effective! In the beginning you might have trouble remembering the affirmation you decided to repeat to yourself. This is an indication of the ego's resistance taking over. So write down your positive affirmations and don't give up until they sink in and become part of your internal makeup.

If you have had difficulty with self-acceptance and acquiring a healthy self-value system, know that it is OK to feel your emotions.

You may attract an unwanted situation due to your affirmations, which are attempting to get your energy in alignment with the chosen goal of your affirmation. Author Teal Swan (discover more about her works in the reference pages at the end of this manual) would have something like this to say about positive affirmations. Positive focus and affirmations are awesome. But remember that with deep traumatic issues your focus tends to be locked into that deep trauma. Your issues (traumas) are most likely tied into your personal clipboard of reasons for incarnation and you are here on Earth to resolve those issues. Your subconscious and conscious minds are often focused on your issues, whether you realize it or not. The unwanted situations you attract during life are attracted to you to give you the opportunity to resolve those pre cognitive issues. That is precisely why most people cannot see how this process works. They are often not aware of the issues they have been born to go beyond because the issues (beliefs) were formed into their psyche before the age of 4! The situations you attract are because of the contents of your mind. If you are experiencing an unwanted attracted situation, remember that these are opportunities to help you resolve the issues in your mind, thoughts and beliefs. If you attempt to eliminate your deep unresolved issues with positive affirmations, you are actually resisting your issues. You are actually focusing on your issues. Without resolve, those issues cannot be erased. To reiterate, as you resist, so shall it persist! Positive focus (affirmations) works for everything, accept for when we use positive focus as our mode of resistance. Positive focus works for anything except for when we are trying to avoid or get away from

110

an issue that needs resolve. If you feel at odds with an affirmation and feel it is getting you nowhere, it may be that the contents of the affirmation is vibrating at a completely different level compared to where you are vibrating. The two energy levels are not a match. The variance is too great and you will only experience unrest when your affirmation exists at a vastly different level as your current state. It is at this moment that a conscious spiritual person will dive into the deeper shadows of the contents of their mind to resolve these hidden issues. This empowering process can seem confusing, daunting and difficult to believe but when at the cross roads named resolve and inner child, it is precisely the time to get help with healing the pre cognitive learned beliefs (memes). Resolving these issues may unfold into learning why you were born! The needs of an imbalanced inner child can make us act in ways that are contrary to what many deem, normal behavior. See Chapter 4 and John Bradshaw's approach concerning where to start healing the inner child.

Once again, emotion is energy in motion and it can be expressed in a safe way, which will allow the emotion to be released. A release of pent up emotion may require you to obtain guidance from a coach or therapist, so that the emotions can be not only fully expressed but also expressed in a safe manner. Know that many of us often hit a wall when attempting to increase our own self-value system, due to never getting a high level of love or acceptance by our parents and other authority figures. Whether the people who raised you are deceased or just ambivalent to your needs, a need for acceptance can often be created. Approval and acceptance are concepts we eventually have to give to ourselves. Seeking it from an outside source is not only difficult but it is never as valid or long lasting as creating internal self-acceptance. When we feel a need for our parents or an authority figures acceptance of us is more important than our own internal acceptance of self, we will be on a never-ending treadmill, and until one increases his own personal acceptance from an internal perspective, one might fail. Give yourself credit for accomplishments, however small and think of them often.

Physically healing oneself is a huge issue for most people on the path because experiencing disease can be an important motivator to begin seeking alternative options. Our western medical approach often takes action to eliminate the symptom rather than healing the cause. It always comes down to raising one's energy, which in turn allows the elimination of the causes of a disease. How does one raise his vibration, you ask? Forgiveness when necessary is paramount. Next, I would suggest a healthy alkaline diet, understand and experience the power of humor and laughing, work with the natural powers of Mother Earth, exercise, acknowledge and slay the internal dragon of negativity, ask the powers that be for help (prayer), seek healers who use energies rather than pills, balance the chakras and take an active part in one's own healing. Please remember that diet plays a huge part in our brains function and will be reflected in our moods, thoughts and physical body.

I am not saying don't go to the doctor or stop taking medication, I am saying look at the options and use them as an adjunct to your healing regime. Disease is often an internal imbalance, an energy block and or a lack of love. There are healers that are connected to spirit. They have, through dedication, harnessed the powers that exist and use these powers for the good of serving others. Only your doubt stands in the way of these healers abilities. I have personally taken part in healing of another by asking like-minded individuals to help channel positive healing powers for another. This action is always taken for the greatest good of all concerned. The resulting healing and communications have been astounding!

In my opinion, in conjunction with the doctor of your choice's treatment, thought is one of, if not the most important place, to begin a healing. But on your walk through life you may want to research alternative methods of healing that can act as an adjunct to changing your internal thought system. Even though the western, scientific outlook concerning these methods is often less then positive, many have used alternative healing processes with very good results. A few of the many optional healing methods that you may want to research are, Reiki, Acupuncture, Cranial Osteopathy, Crystal energy, Massage, Bio-Feedback, Tai Chi, Yoga, Essential Oils, Tapping, and Herbal remedies. High quality pure essential oils for instance can help you to begin taking an active part in addressing any imbalance that has manifested a disease. Man has used essential oils for thousands of years and the leaders in essential oil research have made leaps and bounds in how these essential oils can specifically aid us. One company who is taking a positive approach toward producing pure essential oils and educating the masses on how to use them is Young Living. To give you an idea of how these oils can be used for your benefit, I include a partial list of specific emotions and the recommended antidotal Young Living essential oil, as stated in the book Releasing Emotional Patterns With Essential Oils by Carolyn L. Mein D. C.

Addiction ------------------------------- Peace and Calming

Dizziness ------------------------------- Frankinscense

Fear ------------------------------- Sandalwood

Grief ------------------------------- Joy

Fear of intimacy ------------------- Rose

Sadness ------------------------------- Lemon

Scattered ------------------------------- Idaho Balsam fir

Physical stress ---------------------- Eucalyptus

Please e-mail me and request a FREE aroma pendant with your choice of any one of the above Young Living oils embedded in it. While supply lasts! $4.95 Shipping fee

Or contact me with any questions!
aquarianspiritualdiet@gmail.com

There have been good reports of mentally stressed people experiencing a positive result by using a healing technique called tapping. Tapping can be described as a self administered light tapping on your acupressure points while thinking of a difficult situation you are having trouble with. There are YouTube videos about tapping and Nick Ortner has a book about it called The Tapping Solution.

Michael Sealey can offer powerful, relaxing YouTube hypnosis videos to help identify and lovingly heal your subconscious negative programming. There is a link to one of his YouTube videos in the recommended suggestion list at the end of this manual.

Also, for further reading concerning thoughts in relation to disease, see the recommended reading list for You Can Heal Your Life by Louise Hay and Love Your Disease by John Harrison.

◈Chapter Twenty-One◈
Should I fear what I think?

One must not fear their thoughts. But it is true that you could benefit by monitoring the thoughts and emotions with the intention to remove the ones that are painful, judgmental and fear based. "How do I do this", you ask? If you have any interest in growing as a person and automatically giving this new you and the higher energy you will emit as a gift to the Universe, I suggest you look for and choose alternative beliefs specific to your needs. Like peeling away layers of an onion, discard the thoughts that don't serve you and locate and adopt truths that take steps in a direction toward inner peace.

What is inner peace? It is a lack of worry and fear thoughts, which have been replaced with loving alternatives. Your mind and heart are then working together. It is living in the moment and connecting with your inner you.

A comforting thought is the knowledge that negative thoughts are not as powerful as thoughts surrounded in love. If you catch your negative thoughts about yourself or others and work on them to sway them toward thoughts generated by a more loving, accepting and non-judgmental place, you will see that with repetition the results of the loving thoughts have the strength to override the negative ones. So don't fear your thoughts, embrace the fact that you can observe them. Be grateful for the opportunity to have nurtured this observational awareness. Many people are not aware of the fact that they can do this. They have a thought, they react out of fear, and turmoil is more likely to surround them because of it. Paul McCartney and John Lennon weren't just rock stars. When they said, "All you need is love, love is all you need," they were writing from a higher place and were often not far off base when they sang about spiritual matter in their songs. Listen deeply to the words of Beatles songs such as: All you need is love, Across the Universe, Imagine, and Mother Mary, just to name a few. In my humble opinion, it wasn't by chance that the fab four became one of the most popular and financially successful music groups of all time, after they went to India to study Eastern spiritual ways and introduce those philosophies to the West. It may very well have been part of The Beatles destiny to do so.

The western countries were ready for that information and the mission to help spread the spiritual philosophies had always been on John's, Paul's, George's and Ringo's imaginary clipboard.

⊰Chapter Twenty-Two⊱
How do I determine whether my thoughts
are positive or negative?

Trusting your intuition, emotions and heart felt inner knowing is a fine place to begin determining the positive or negative quality of your thoughts. Become the observer of your thoughts. Use your uncomfortable emotional states as a warning flag to check out the thoughts that are currently generating these uncomfortable emotions. When you stop and look within, you are then in a better position to choose alternative thoughts. Be the watcher. Are your thoughts detrimental to anything or anyone? Are they thoughts you would be comfortable thinking about yourself, or would they make you uncomfortable? If you have thoughts generated out of anger, judgment, insecurity, distrust, self-criticism, hate, vengeance, or control over another, based on wants and needs rather than unconditional love, you are generating thoughts that would be considered low vibrational thoughts and negative. When possessing these human thought patterns it indicates you would benefit from introspection and the seeking out of alternative more loving thoughts. Understand that if you are generating a thought that comes from a non-loving emotion such as anger, you are in an ego-based negative thought process. You might say "if I can't scream obscenities at that stupid driver that cut me off I will go mad!" The point being, you are already a tad mad. At that point, you are in an uncontrollable negative emotional state and it would be in your best interest to heal your internal anger, rather than feel justified in that so-called needed scream. In such a case, you have targeted another to be the recipient of your emotional imbalance and have been given the opportunity to heal yourself, rather than choosing to be stagnated in your painful thoughts. Don't just force your emotion away or bury it deep down. Control, rather then addressing the emotional issue, will not solve the emotional problem. You must address the emotion and learn to balance it or this stifled emotion might very well manifest in a future medical problem in your body.

First know that if you are not at a place of inner peace when generating thoughts, the thoughts you generate are serving you in a positive way only from the standpoint of offering the opportunity to change yourself. An example would be, if you are angry when driving your car and getting mad at other drivers, it's quite possible that you may have emotional problems that could be addressed. Check out the New Mood Therapy book by David Burns in the recommended book section. Second, try this driving experience experiment. When you are driving and you are seemingly late, in a great hurry and quite possibly out of balance, do you seem to attract red lights, slow drivers or situations that will slow you down? If so, take a deep cleansing breath, let your shoulders drop, look within yourself for a non-rushed attitude, adopt it and know without a doubt that all will be well. Change your inner need to rush thoughts, to a thought such as "I will get

118

there in time." If you can truly change your state and energy pattern you will be amazed at how things will work out. The slow car in front of you will make a turn or the person that you are meeting will call and say, "I will be 15 minutes late, is that OK?" Or if you are really in a high state of vibration, you will be amazed that you arrive several minutes before you thought was physically possible! Remember that any thought generated from fear is going to be a thought that is not in your best interest. When you are strong enough to challenge your current negative thought system and seek out positive alternatives, you will discover mental freedoms. It is the higher road to take, rather then thinking something is wrong with you. An example of a self-defeating situation would be the refusal to talk to a therapist by a person who is in mental agony, depressed, with traits of overwhelming sadness, low self-esteem, anger, or any trait that keeps them in a less then peaceful state. Some might feel useless and defective by admitting their condition to a therapist. To the contrary, it is a wise and courageous person that knows to look within for thoughts that could be changed for the better.

Medical issues such as a thyroid imbalance can be treated from a medical standpoint but should simultaneously be treated from a thought-system approach. Mental therapy, chakra balancing, acupuncture, massage, reiki, essential oils, meditation, possible mineral deficiency, exercise and self hypnosis are just a few of the ways you can help change your thoughts, change your medical condition, and therefore heighten your energy. To remove and change some of these non-serving thoughts will be a wonderful gift to yourself. There is always hope, don't ever think you are alone or defective. We are ALL, I repeat, ALL working on something and we are all in this journey called life, together. Make the mature decision to become responsible for yourself and internal mind.

Nurture a safe loving place for your inner child. When you do, you will become more aware of your mission in this life, lessen your fear and take positive steps toward creating what your heart tells you is the proper path.

The seven major chakra locations

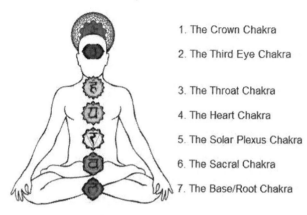

1. The Crown Chakra

2. The Third Eye Chakra

3. The Throat Chakra

4. The Heart Chakra

5. The Solar Plexus Chakra

6. The Sacral Chakra

7. The Base/Root Chakra

⋖Chapter 23⋗
What is a chakra?

There are seven major energy centers on the human body and thousands of minor energy points located from head to toe. These seven major centers are called Chakras. The acupuncturists, among others, understand these areas allow the flow of energy through these points. One of the major functions of the acupuncturist is to allow proper energy flow through these points. When any of your seven major energy centers (Chakras) are blocked or out of alignment, an imbalance in your energy flow and health will manifest in direct proportion to the imbalance.

Eastern medicine has understood for thousands of years that if you have a health issue, it is wise to treat the imbalance rather then only the symptom. Meditation and visualization can be used in order to help maintain personal balance as you align your Chakra system. There are Chakra balancing CD's and healing practitioners that can help you to understand how to balance the energy points (Chakras) of the body. Seeking out a healing practitioner can also be helpful when you have difficulty entering an area of your mental makeup that is hard to pin point or is hidden.

After a Chakra balance meditation, consult your inner makeup, body and thoughts. Have the negative thoughts been diminished? Do you feel energized? Do you find unresolved issues? Have issues reared their ugly head as if to say, "deal with this?" If you do notice reactions such as these, know that as you heal specific inner imbalance or negativity, you will eventually raise your energy and find new freedoms. If you discover positive reactions to your Chakra work, know that these subtle exercises can be layered over each other and as they overlap, they will grow and begin to help you raise your energy. Take an active part in balancing the Chakra system and as you gain more energy and balance, you can use this energetically higher mental state to courageously confront negative internal thought systems. A Chakra balance meditation is a wonderful place to begin walking that razors edge. The razors edge is a metaphor for how easy it is to fall one way toward negativity, stay balanced on the thin edge or fall onto the side of positivity. The world around you will begin to seem a better place, when in fact it is a reflection of your inner being as a result of your more positive balanced thoughts and balanced Chakra energy system. They go hand in hand.

Dysfunction will lower your energy, so take a look at alternative healing ways to replace those old negative systems of thought. You have read several times to replace your negative thoughts and may find yourself asking "but how"? Each of us is different with respect to what our internal mental make-up is filled with.

By using this manual as a guide to understanding answers to the "why" question, you can better understand where to begin in regards to changing negative thoughts to loving ones. Use your intuition as you read and re-read this manual and then consult the recommended reading section. Ask "is there a book from this section that I identified with"? Does one of the recommended books, cd's or videos stand out as an important place to start?

My words are attempting to make you aware of the tools

available in order to unravel the beliefs that might be holding you back both mentally and physically. It is inevitably up to you to decide to take a look within. You get to choose when you will begin a process of removing the negativity, healing, embracing positivity, and allowing love.

✥Chapter Twenty-Four✥
Is there a difference between vibration and energy?

Every atom in the Universe is energy and has a vibrational rate. Our thoughts have energy behind them. Vibration and energy can be considered virtually synonymous. They are closely related and almost interchangeable. We generate higher vibrations with loving positive thoughts and feelings, while negative thoughts create the opposite. We are often unaware negative thoughts create toxic energy blocks within the body, mind and spirit. Our energetic self emits thoughts or signals and will attract whatever is in harmony with the vibration of those thoughts. Since positive loving thoughts have a higher frequency of vibration, when we think them, we will attract higher vibrational beings, material things and situations into our frame of awareness. An example would be a loving thought about another person that is non-controlling and based on unconditional love. Such a thought wants nothing from the other person but is generated from a giving mind-set. This thought would be a higher vibratory thought that will result in giving off positive energy. When you are a giving non-judgmental, loving, fearless being, you are going to vibrate at a high level. Your thoughts will have more energy then a negative person. Similar vibrations will attract and the situations you will experience while giving that unconditional love, will attract more of the same into your life. A higher vibrational being will never think he is a victim. He may never have accidents. He will arrive at the intersection where a car accident occurred, ten minutes before

123

or after it has happened. His vibration was not a match to the lower accident-prone vibration of the persons involved in the accident. A simple test of this is when you are accident prone and drop that light bulb or let the quart of milk slip out of your hand; take a moment to center yourself. Look within to identify the mind-set that was not serving you well. Take a deep slow breath, slow down and find a balanced state of mind. Begin to release those emotional states created from a rushed "not in the moment" frustration level of mind. Change those identified negative thoughts you started with, relax and change them around. Now that you are feeling a bit more centered and in a higher vibrational state, observe if the accidents slow down or cease to happen. Now smile, you just learned a great deal about thought energy and vibration. As you observe this change in your reality you will find a truth or validation in the knowing it is helpful to be aware of your mindset and change negative to positive thoughts.

Since we possess energy within our bodies, it is a simple jump to find truth in the fact that we can help control the flow of energy within the body. A book that takes us back to basics and to understand the balancing powers of the earth is <u>To Be Healed by the Earth</u> by Warren Grossman. Grossman's book can offer you a healing direction that most are not even aware of. Mother Earth is alive with energy and we should not only respect Mother Earth, but also ask permission to use her power to create balance within each of us.

To become familiar with Mother Earth's healing powers, studying and applying techniques from Grossman's book is a wonderful place to begin understanding that natural energy. **#15**

As you adopt a spiritual path that allows a conscious journey toward true connection to Source, know that such a journey never ends. This will allow you to drop the negative anxious thoughts that can result from being dissatisfied with your progress, or wishes for a quicker journey. Allow the petals of your inner being blossom at their own rate and simultaneously be thankful they are unfolding. Know that a spiritual journey is a never-ending journey and become comfortable with your current state of being and evolution.

The use of verbal or silently spoken positive affirmations

can also begin to open doors of positive possibility and help change your energy. An affirmation example is the mirror exercise that Louise Hay often recommends. That is where you get up, walk to the mirror, look into your eyes and say to yourself, "I love and approve of myself." This may sound silly or useless until a person who may have challenges with liking himself finds that he has difficulty with such an exercise. Repetition of positive affirmations in areas you find challenges can help. As you begin to know and believe the positive affirmations and mentally adopt their content, positive results will begin to show up in your reality. Once the use of positive affirmation has begun, it is useful to discover what related fearful thought might exist within the mind that needs to be replaced with a more loving thought. That negative thought or belief will stand in the way of your affirmation taking root in your mind. When the replacement takes place the new more loving thought will manifest as the new you. New more positive experiences will enter your world.

Truths can be discovered in a flash as a revelation, a quick jump through the Satori window and quickly alter your reality and vibration whereas other shifts can take decades to unwind. It is our ego's resistance to changing the fearful thoughts to loving thoughts that often determines the speed of mental change.

Becoming aware of the ego's resistance, while increasing the strength of your conscious choice, will reduce the egos power over you. Remember that the ego is closely related to your early childhood adopted memes. These memes are what often need healing to go beyond their limitations. This will be a benefit to your peaceful unfolding.

Your left brain is the analytical side of the brain and it may be able to read and somewhat understand a new positive idea or affirmation, but until you make a choice to make the idea part of your life, it may remain elusive. It's a good idea to write this wanted trait on paper or your bathroom mirror, re-read it often and hold an honest willingness for change. The same holds true when working on raising your level of self-love. Write down your positive traits or accomplishments, no matter how huge or small these items may seem. Read your positive traits list often, especially when your ego is challenging your worthiness. You can also ask Source for help by asking (praying) what you are supposed to learn from your current experiences and help with understanding this current opportunity. It is often uncanny how a simple affirmation can elude our mind until it becomes ingrained into the thought system. The false-self or ego usually resists the death of a fearful thought and will fight to have the old trait stay alive. Not until your resistance has diminished, often from a simultaneous conscious effort to increase your inner energy, that a shift in consciousness occurs and the new thought becomes part of your mental makeup. This shift in consciousness will make this new concept a truth. Mediation or self-hypnosis can also aid in your transformation. This doesn't always have to be in internal battle. At minimum the practice of meditation and hypnosis can give your negative state a rest in order to increase your energy and begin to gain a new perspective. A word of caution concerning meditation might be appropriate here. Be careful not to overuse these meditative practices as an escape, which could possibly prolong your forward progression. Issues do not go away until resolve is complete.

Once again, it is important to remember that this journey from fear to love never ends. Do not feel rushed, or your imbalance may manifest a difficult learning situation. It can be helpful when you are having difficulty releasing a fear or having difficulty identifying a negative trait to say to the forces that be "I am willing to change, what am I supposed to learn from this current situation?" Then watch and listen for the answers, as the answer can show up instantly or in mysterious ways.

Questions, interaction and positive growth can arise in very strong and powerful ways when a group of like-minded individuals come together. So seek out spiritually inclined companions to help each other when exploring loving freedoms. This is what is meant when the Bible states "for where two or three are gathered in my name, there I am among them". Each one of us is on this spiritual growth quest whether we know it or not. Growth never ends, so take it in stride and be grateful for the steps you have taken toward mental freedoms, inner peace and closeness to Source. It is my humble opinion that even God continues to grow through us and embraces the love that we find.

So be proud of your spiritual growth, it is your gift to all that is, even God. Re-read and re-listen to your spiritually inclined material often and repeatedly. As you recognize and drop negative internal traits, thoughts shift toward a more loving mental system. This same material you read or listened to a few months earlier will offer new insights! It's not that the material changed, you did. You may have not been ready for the shift that the material offered. It is amazing how you can re-read something at a later date and say to yourself after a revelation has been experienced, "wow I didn't seem to read that the first time around!"

If you ask for change and the challenges that arise become to difficult, ask (pray) for the challenge to slow down. You might want to take a break from your new adopted life of increasing your energy and experience a vacation of sorts. Take a needed break once in a while and re-center yourself before re-approaching your spiritual growth.

Whether you call it vibration or energy, the act of understanding its existence, is a wonderful revelation.

Comprehending what can be accomplished with vibration and energy opens up a unique realm of possibility.

❧Twenty-five❧
What is karma?

Mr. Miyagi from <u>The Karate Kid</u> movie was wise when he said, "Must have balance Daniel-son!" He was aware that everything must have balance. Karma is the balancing of energy given off by everything. A can of beans sealed in a vacuum has air rushing in when opened. This is a direct result from the air pressure attempting to balance itself. This is balance or karma. The basic theory is cause and affect.

When a person generates energy through intention, thought and action he will eventually attract a learning opportunity in order to further understand his past actions. It is his right to experience the same. This creates an opportunity to choose a more loving action the next time around. A more definitive example would be if you harm another a similar action or situation would be attracted to you to balance out your karma. "What goes around comes around" is another saying that is attempting to define karma. This applies to good intentions and actions, as well. Even though it might seem that your past actions or intentions might be karmatically responsible for unwanted situations in your present life, it is wise to know that your karma can instantly change in direct proportion to how you change your internal mindset, forgive and create true shifts in consciousness. Unskilled or negative thought patterns such as anger, blame or guilt might cause a continuation of unwanted karmic situations. As Dr. Wayne Dyer used to say, "Change your thoughts, change your life." **#16**

To make peace with your karma, **be thankful** for your past experiences and **take responsibility** for manifesting them. A release of blame and adopting true forgiveness are gifts you give to yourself. It is truly a huge step for one on the seekers path to understand how karma works and guides their thought, intention and actions on how karma can be played out. You can have a negative intention while creating a pleasant action. If your intention was a selfish one, you are not creating positive karma.

Being thankful for all past experiences allows you to understand that you have been given a gift of awakening to the peaceful powers of God and love. The Universe understood it was time for you to awaken and gave you the opportunity for accelerated positive transformation. Everything in your past has been dealt with by you in the best way you could, based on your abilities. As you look back on the past, know that everything that has happened was to give you opportunities to grow and become a better person.

Gratitude is a very loving thought pattern and once you are grateful compared to blaming another, self blame, or fear of negative karma, you are on the way to taking a step toward being one with Source. The Buddhists would say "may you be happy, may you be well" and may you be peaceful. Nowhere in those three thoughts are there any wishes that you seek revenge or think less of yourself by getting stuck with a thought system that sees yourself with anything but love.

≈Chapter Twenty-Six≈
What is the significance of fear and love?

Absolutely everything in this world starts is existence from either a basis out of <u>fear</u> or a basis out of <u>love</u>. All thought, intention and action originates from those two driving forces. But you say what about hate? Hate arises when a person feels threatened by something or someone and judgments are made. Fear begets the thoughts of being threatened. People who harbor fear-based thought often don't have a clue that a trusting, loving approach could heal their insecurity and the hate would dissipate.

This universe is founded on the principle that love solves everything. It's really that simple. It is our ego, insecurities, fears, anxieties, mistrust, judgments, lack of healthy self-love, and unbalanced emotions that make it difficult.

True unconditional love asks for nothing, it is a giving all-powerful force. Most relationships are based on needs and wants, not love. Mutual attraction or karma can play a role in connecting people, but most relationships are conditional. When the ego doesn't agree with the spouse's thoughts or actions, one falls out of so called love to prove their point. Such is an example of a response, which is generated from needs and wants. The more love you give the more love you will receive. Such a concept is a basis for the future of humanity to ponder. You give it and you get more back! You can never run out of love, so don't worry about its overuse!

These days it seems that many people want something from you. It is truly a wonderful thing to know you can gain by giving. That's a beautiful example to contemplate concerning the all-powerful force of karma! Karma is responding to your intentions as well as actions. It is truly a loving person who can create good karma while giving unconditionally. It is when good karma is expected or an act is played out with conditions where good karma can be negated.

Recently we are beginning to observe a new wave of businesses that contribute all or part of their profits to charity. Be observant of this trend of social entrepreneurship, as it will be a needed step in the next phase of Capitalism. I believe social entrepreneurism will be mandatory to allow Capitalism to evolve to its next phase. **#17**

Tom's Shoes is a business that was on the forefront of this movement.

If you can honestly analyze fear and love, which are the two main driving forces in the Universe, attempt to identify anything you have observed which doesn't have its origin in either. You will discover this to be a worthwhile but often difficult, if not impossible process.

◆Chapter Twenty-Seven◆

Is it true that I must love myself before

I can truly love others?

Yes.

Self-love and self-esteem are the greatest gifts you can give yourself. Feeling good about who you are in a non-narcissistic way is a good thing. It builds confidence and allows you to come to the realization that you are part of the God Force or the Tao. When you do not like yourself or have a lack of self-esteem, you will find yourself manipulating people and things to suit your shortcomings. You might compensate by seeking the best looking wife, the biggest automobile, a large house, being desperate by overt or subliminal asking for approval, needing other worth from praise, (other worth is deriving your self-value by getting praise from another) the finest designer clothes, scents, material possessions and the list goes on and on. As Dr. Wayne Dyer had said, "when you define yourself by what you do or what you have, when they are gone, you aren't!" **#18** As you begin to like and love yourself more, you will then begin to truly know what it is to like and love another. Start by building your internal value system by concentrating on your accomplishments and attributes. Think supportive thoughts often, while minimizing those internal repetitive negative thoughts about yourself, and eventually shift those thoughts to an internal love of self, just because you are. True self-love isn't based on accomplishments or things, but rather on a connection to Source and a knowing you are part of that Source.

Divorce is prevalent in America due to the fact that many relationships are based on needs and wants. Divorce is as easy as throwing away a defective appliance when your relationship is based on such a premise. Your needs and wants make demands on the other person. It is wise to be aware of the effects of true unconditional love and it's resulting good karma. You cannot possibly have a blissful marriage when the relationship is based on needs and wants. Relationships based on needs and wants are a take, take, take situation. Successful relationships are ones based on giving without expectation. The more you give, the more you shall receive. This receiving happens when you have a relationship based on true unconditional love rather than conditions. When exploring what unconditional love is, study the word "allowing." It is true unconditional love that "allows" the significant other to do, be, grow, let go, experience and act in any way they feel a need to. If a partner acts in a manner that is not beneficial to the stability or growth of the marriage, that act can be explored. At that point the couple can discuss optional choices to establish a new direction.

When one develops true self-value he is in a position of mental strength, which in turn allows positive relationships with others.

⋖Chapter Twenty-Eight⋗
How can I learn to meditate and love my-self more?

Meditation and taking an active part in increasing your self-value system often go hand in hand. The use of self-hypnosis CDs, lectures plus meditational materials on how to increase your self-value system can be very helpful and can be found in the resources sections of this book.

In order to increase your personal self-image, begin by stopping all self-criticism. To increase your self-value a reprogramming of your basic internal belief system, may also be necessary. Another helpful tool is the use of affirmations. These are positive sayings you speak out-loud and or silently over and over until they begin to take root in your thought system. Louise Hay is a great teacher when it comes to affirmations, as was Stuart Wilde. Using affirmations can get your brain to begin to accept your new, kinder thoughts about yourself. In order to begin changing your internal less then positive thought patterns, start by challenging the beliefs you were told as a child. Understand that it is all right to forgive your parents, teachers and other authority figures that influenced you, if you are of the opinion that they didn't do a good job. They did the best they knew how, at that moment in time.

A great time of the day to heal and reprogram is just before sleep by using self-hypnosis, dedication or affirmations. Use the time sleeping for putting good thoughts into your mind. Some reprogramming CDs are designed to relax you and listen to before sleep, while others are subliminal and can help change your self-criticism to positive mental thoughts about yourself while you go about your daily actions or while in a deep sleep.

There are four main vibrational states your brain exists in. The conscious or beta brain wave state, the alpha or relaxed state, deeper yet, the theta, and then comes delta, the deeply relaxed or sleep-mode state. All four can be accessed and re-programmed. To become more positive, you might have to challenge your beliefs while in any of these four states. By using all four states to change your thoughts to more positive content, you will be challenging your conscious and subconscious mind.

Another way to begin your quest for self-esteem and inner peace is by meditating. Meditation demands some mental practice, as the jumpy never ceasing monkey mind is often difficult to slow down and shut off. Meditation is basically learning not to think as often as we do, learning to relax and live in the moment. Learning to go into a deep state of mind by releasing internal thought and still remain awake is also a practiced form of meditation. It is a letting go, not an action. Meditation can help you physically, mentally, and reduces stress. While in a meditative state, your affirmations and visualizations become more powerful as you are concentrating your thought and circumventing your conscious filters. When in deep meditation, you are closer to where the barriers between the different levels of mind are thin. Such a mental state is where you are able to connect with Source or guidance. By stating a positive **intention** or dedication before meditating, your meditation can take on a deeper meaning. The meditation's intention might be seeking an answer to a question about a current life lesson. The intention might be asking for help

135

with a healing or to become closer to source. The possibilities of intention are endless and when you become aware of your **intentions** of any act, whether it be a meditative one or a conscious one, you become more aware of the answer to that big "WHY" question, which is so important in unraveling our imbalances.

Source is always available, as you are a part of Source, but it is by meditating and removing the thoughts of the everyday beta conscious mind, which creates access to your higher-self, become more possible. Connecting with Source by removing the selfish "I" is one of the positive results of meditation. It also has the potential to reduce the often painful egos hold on your everyday existence.

There are many ways to begin a meditation practice. I recommend researching the methods that resonate with you. Here and in the resources section on recommended reading, I offer a few methods to begin your journey inward. Dedicate 10 minutes everyday to get up early or whatever time period works for you. The key here is to circumvent the ego's resistance to meditation. You may find yourself succumbing to excuses as to why you can't dedicate these 10 minutes on any particular day. Here is where your choice, dedication, free will and steadfast fortitude need to be strengthened. Do whatever is necessary to do this 10 minutes exercise, EVERYDAY. Whenever possible find a quiet peaceful place that can be accessed on a daily basis. This space can actually take on energy from your attempts to get quiet, so use the same space as often as possible. The space will eventually help you by reflecting back its peaceful offering, in direct relation to how much positive energy you emit while in that space. Sit with your back straight, which will allow a better flow of energy within the body. Take a pencil, paper, timer and a candle or oil lamp into the space with you. Light the candle in a safe place and set it just above eye level and out in front of where you will be seated. Take three slow deep breaths and dedicate that breath energy to your guides, your mind, body and spirit, your higher self or whatever you think could benefit from the energy emitted from your conscious breathing. Start the 10-minute timer and forget about it. During this 10 minute timed period, stare at the candle flame. Be the watcher of your thoughts. Relax, let go, concentrate on the candle flame, be the light. Let your thoughts drift away. If you catch a recurring thought, transform it into a geometric shape of choice, place it into a golden bubble and let it drift away like a small white puffy cloud caught in a gentle breeze. Know that you will be able to retrieve that thought at a later time. Eventually your eyes will not jump around or off the flame. When your eyes jump around, gently bring your attention back to the flame. As you watch the candle and without watching the paper, rest your pencil on the paper. Make one pencil mark on the paper every time you are interrupted by a sound, or a thought. Become aware of anytime you are not without thought. These interruptions will make you aware of the monkey mind, the ego, and the inner resistance to being calm and still. Stop this exercise when the timer goes off. Date your sheets of marked paper and do this candle exercise everyday! After a few weeks, compare the quantity of paper marks. You will be delighted that you are learning to quiet the mind, or at minimum get some good relaxation. In time, you will be able to take control over your consciousness and lower the quantity of pencil marks during those 10-minute meditations. As you let go and learn not to fight or chastise yourself concerning the interruptions, you will be on your way to experiencing your inner worlds.

In an attempt to take your meditative practice to the next step, try to sit quietly in your dedicated meditation space, take three dedicated breaths, as discussed above. Close your eyes and become aware of your rhythmic breathing. Do not force the breathing process or consciously slow it down. Just be aware of the process. Count one as you breathe in. Count two as you breathe out. Do this until you reach ten and then start over at one. As thoughts enter your mind don't fight them just release them as you entertain becoming as solid as a mountain. You are steadfast as a mountain. Let your thoughts drift away as lazy clouds might pass in the sky. Let your shoulders, scalp, muscles around the eyes and your entire body relax. Eventually you will quiet the mind and counting becomes unnecessary. Enjoy your mental vacation. Meditation takes practice but the benefits are often mandatory for true connection to Source. You can dedicate the meditation, ask for guidance or ask to become closer to Source. Then as you become still, listen. During meditations, answers often appear. A great book to learn about meditation and more is called Turning Your Mind Into An Ally by Pema Chodron.

One of the greatest realizations one can come to regarding a boost to your value system and love yourself more, is that you are part of Source. You see the Tao, Source, God, Force or whatever you would like to call it, exists everywhere in everything, so you have to conclude that it is also in you. In a non-narcissistic ego-less way, acceptance of the fact that you are part of this Source energy allows you to strip away the limiting thoughts you were brought up to believe. In my humble opinion as we change thoughts of fear to thoughts of love, we are taking part in the never-ending blossoming process of God. Your progression toward positive loving thought is helping God grow the power of love. This is all part of the unfolding, spiritual journey.

Affirmations such as "I approve of myself" are powerful words and thoughts. Stuart Wilde would have you say and eventually believe, "I am eternal, immortal, universal, and infinite, I am power." As you say words such as these out loud and to yourself repetitively everyday and before sleep, you begin to raise your vibration and attain a higher state of self-love and confidence. A great test to determine your level of your current self-value system is to say affirmations such as "I completely love and approve of myself" as you look into your eyes while gazing in a mirror. Observe your reaction, as you verbalize the affirmation to yourself. Was there a tendency to look away or disbelieve the words you are speaking to yourself? Do you have trouble remembering the exact wording of an affirmation? If so, it might be in your best interest to continue with such affirmations. When non-narcissistic true self-love eludes you and you seek a clarification on the subject, I can highly recommend listening to the lecture on How To Love Yourself by Louise Hay. A link to the Hay House page to access this lecture is in the resources.

⊰Chapter Twenty-Nine⊱
What is the meaning of life?

The truths are quite simple but here is the twist. In many cases what our soul signs up for and what we are exposed to as children by our parents and formal education, often teaches us lack of self-love, judgment, fear and the safeness of conformity. Participation in actions of competition then teaches us a need to be better than others. Through fear we learn to judge others to boost our false ego. We as humans have lost our connection to Source and instead attempt to feel better about ourselves by participating in acts that belittle others. Evidence of these belittling judgmental acts can be found in the workplace, in the political arena, on the world's highways, and on many sports fields when judgment of those who appear different or dangerous to us occurs based on a personal bias. Most humans feel a need to be number one or superior to another. This is a throwback to the barbaric and ancient hierarchy of class systems, Emperors, and Kings. These accepted low opinions led to false superiority that was evident when early man participated in sports like actions in the Roman Coliseum and before that in the Greek Olympic games. Yes, it is true that modern humans have accomplished wonderful feats of physicality with their bodies thru dedication and sports participation but when one analyzes the quite often prevalent motivation behind those accomplishments, one often learns the basic truths as to the "WHY" they began such a sports quest in the first place. Why does a boxer, wrestler, or football player attempt to physically beat his opponent? It is often to feel better about himself and to feel superior or number one. He has been conditioned to think it is OK to hurt another to gain a false sense of self, release negative emotions and show physical superiority. Often he is rewarded monetarily for doing so. These monetary rewards and school scholarships perpetuate these types of competitive sports because there is money to be made. The sportsman is being used for making a profit and becomes a pawn involved with the continuation of basic negative human traits. Is this much different from when the lions and gladiators fought in front of Roman Emperors? What often happens when a sports player gets older and becomes number two, is that "he/she" feels horrible. What happens when one can't play sports anymore? One will often feel less of themselves. Through actions on the field, they are attempting to feed the ego. As Dr. Wayne Dyer said, "When you are what you do, or are what you have, when you can't do or you don't have, you aren't." The twist is that such beliefs based on thoughts of a false self-value based on possessions or accomplishments are generated by the ego and stand in the way of witnessing the truths. Conversely, when a person becomes close to Source and knows that we are all one, he begins his walk toward inner peace and learns to love himself. He learns that serving others is vastly more satisfying then winning. He has no driving need to feed the false self by beating another, for as he beats another he realizes he is beating himself. An unbalanced intention toward competition is less productive then having fun and enjoying life. There are many positive intentions to participate in sports. Choose your intention wisely. Is it possible to go beyond your needs and wants by connecting to Source? Absolutely. As you eliminate the self-defeating thoughts generated by fear you begin to touch on your magnificence and at the same time, also remain humble. What I am referring to is that the ego sometimes needs to be broken and the false power reduced, such as a wild horse might be tamed to allow this Source connection to truly become evident. A short film that can help one understand how to remain humble is The Powers of Ten by Charles and Ray Eames. Another great watch to see how upset an ego-based person can become when their beliefs systems are challenged is a movie called The Man From Earth, written by Jerome Bixby.

If you find yourself getting a tad edgy about the contents of this chapter, ready to rebut or justify with a knee jerk verbal defensive reaction, you are probably accessing your ego and fear based thoughts. Introspection could help, if you are truly honest with yourself. Some will often staunchly defend such thoughts about the positive aspects of competition and being better by belittling another. If such a person challenged their beliefs about competition, they would feel less about themselves and their accomplishments. Those conflicting thoughts can create a mental bind that is difficult to identify, get past, and heal. To ascertain if you are such a person you might look within your beliefs to help identify the cause or need to indentify with being number one. Why does common man have a huge desire to identify with a winning entity or team? It's often self-value related. If this need gets too strong it can be overtaken by the ego and in some cases drive one to kill another, if another is supporting the opposing team. This has happened when huge crowds of soccer fans get out of control.

Now, I am the first to admit that George Carlin was an unbalanced, angry man but he did have insights as no other. Although he was being very judgmental when he said this quote, he did attempt to see the truth when he said, "Never underestimate the power of stupid people in large groups." These out of balance groups of people feed off each other's imbalances and tend to become one destructive power. This is another example of the power of thought and connected human consciousness. Have you seen that child on the sports playground

141

yelling, "watch me daddy!" This is a plea to continue the growth of the false-self. The child may already have a need for acceptance due to doubts about his true internal worth. If we react to that child by praising him for his playground antics, he is on his way to becoming addicted to the false-self or growth of the ego. Conversely when that child yells "watch me daddy" and we reply, "I enjoy seeing you do that and I enjoy seeing you having fun", we have verbalized to the child our positive reaction, rather than feeding his false-self through empty praise. Personally I currently don't spend much time watching sports but I did play sports for exercise and attempts at defining who I was, in my youth. I was hoping someone would think me a better person by seeing my sports accomplishments. I now use my time for other actions, most which have to do with solitary exercise, yoga, creative pursuits, positive change, writing, time spent with nature, meditation, connection with Source, and time with interesting people. I am once again not saying that sports are right or wrong. I am recommending the WHY question for any action.

Here on Earth we have chosen to incarnate on a planet that consists of many contrasts. Without such, there would be no way to choose and use our free-will to build and grow our souls character. I mention these contrasts to help you see how personal introspection can offer optional mental makeup. Everything is a choice, when you begin to be aware that you are the captain of your soul. One might want to ask, how far do I want to progress my soul, during this lifetime? The answer to this question might offer motivation for change.

Connection to the Source of all things is possible and a simple wonderful truth. But it is our thoughts, which can stand in the way. As Stuart Wilde used to say "Life wasn't meant to be a struggle." It's often our limiting, ego generated low self-esteem thoughts that stand in front of our magnanimous true-self. That is why the experiences here on Earth can be challenging. We generate and attract the experiences we need through the law of attraction by thinking our thoughts, in order to have the opportunity to use our free-will to choose love-generated changes within our minds. Those changes, if made, will not only allow us to grow and never need that same experience again, but will allow the Force to grow simultaneously. If you choose to remain in the same thought pattern that generated the challenging experience in the first place, you will generate that situation again and again and again. That self-generated challenging experience might come at you in a slightly different way each time, but they will all be similar and all offer you the same opportunity for change.

To know we are part of God and on a journey back home is more than a comforting thought. As you drop the limiting fear-based, ego-feeding thoughts and adopt a loving God like thought, voila, you now know the meaning of life. You see it's not all about the egos need to be superior to another, acquiring stuff, or to beat your opponent and accomplish more then someone else. A more beneficial approach is loving yourself and others, as Jesus said, "Love your neighbor as yourself." When you die you cannot take anything with you except the vibrational thoughts that accomplished an elimination of fear and the growth of love that you were able to generate this time around. Now that's a worthy goal. You get to take the love! You will find empowerment through love, not empowerment by making someone else seem less. Here is another lyrical Beatles example," Love is all you need, love is all you need, love is all you need." "Love, Love Love." Another Beatles lyric comes to mind "The love you take is equal to the love you make."

Since this is a vibrational Universe and you vibrate from the quality of your energy, it is a fact that as you release fear, self-doubt and judgmental thoughts and change from within concerning such thoughts, you increase your vibration. As you increase to a higher vibration, you will attract people that reflect your higher vibration, more abundance and better circumstances flow into your life. It's really quite simple. You are a creator, you choose and decide what you want, the power of the Universe has to provide what you want. This is called the Law of Attraction. There are many reference materials, which can help you understand the Law of Attraction. Please see the recommended book list for sources. The speed at how those previously mentioned choices would manifest is in direct proportion to how close you are in alignment to those choices, within your thoughts.

You must be in vibrational harmony with the choices you

143

have made for them to manifest. What does that mean? It means the only things that separate you from instantly manifesting your choices are the thoughts, beliefs and feelings you possess. Those internal attributes will contribute and determine your level of vibration. If you are not in alignment with your choices, or vibrate at the same frequency, your inner being will have to change in order to allow the choices you have made to come into your life. Let me give you an example; you want a close meaningful relationship but you don't love yourself very deeply. You lack confidence and you doubt your self-value. Such a meaningful relationship will not be attracted to the vibrations you are emanating. You will most likely not manifest the meaningful relationship you would prefer, but rather manifest what might seem, as it's opposite. You will, however, attract situations that will allow you to make new choices concerning how much you like yourself. If you watch for these opportunities instead of becoming a victim from them and grow in a positive way, you will change your life's circumstances. These seemingly negative situations may be difficult to face at first, but when looked at as an observer might or in retrospect, they will show how that lesson was a turning point for the better. You will be confused concerning your circumstances and often blame others unless you understand what your internal makeup is, how it affects what you attract to yourself and how changing your internal makeup for the better can or did change your life in a good way. If you constantly make choices that are not in line with your level of vibration, you will be in a constant state of unrest, as the Universe will send you challenge after challenge to help you drop the unwanted lower vibrational traits, which in turn, allow you to choose freeing, higher vibrational traits and thoughts. This always involves dropping the fear-based egocentric thoughts and replacing them with simpler, non-judgmental loving thoughts.

When you are attempting internal change it is good to be aware of the fact that if you excessively abuse alcohol and drugs to alleviate your mental discomforts, you might prolong your journey toward inner peace. Your energy is lowered by overuse of alcohol and drugs. They both act as a band-aid to your internal fears and satiate your level of comfortability with your mental state. This

144

false sense of comfort keeps you from making the internal changes, which can access a more loving, higher energy mindset. The occasional minimal use of alcohol for recreation seems to be condoned by some spiritual teachers but when they are used for escape, when you can't control your intake or when it has power over you, it is working against your spiritual growth. When they are overused they have the power over you and the results can sometimes eventually be fatal.

Being grateful for everything you have and have experienced is a powerful key to increasing your vibration. If you need to better understand this "being grateful" concept or to open up your emotions to learn how to be grateful, use the Internet and Google "Louis Schwartzberg TED talk", concerning nature, beauty and gratitude. **#19** or if it is still available download Panache Desai's free being grateful wave file. **#20**

I have heard it said that, "Sometimes the bad things that happen in our lives, put us directly on the path to the best things that will ever happen to us." My advice in regards to this statement is; "it is when you can make the shift from labeling your past experiences as bad, to accepting those experiences as gifts, that true change and great happenings can be born. Give thanks for those experiences and take responsibility for manifesting them. A release of blame and adopting true forgiveness are gifts you give to yourself."

As always, your inner mental makeup, thoughts and intentions create what surrounds you in the form of what you have attracted into your life. Take personal responsibility for everything you have attracted and learn how to change from within to see how your life will unfold in new and wonderful ways. As you connect with Source, reduce the ego's hold over your inner being, and increase your self-love, you will begin to understand that you are not flawed. You will discover that you don't necessarily need fixing, you just need to be grateful, love yourself, everyone else, and everything that you have attracted into your life, to have the life you desire.

If you are experiencing physical or mental unrest, your separation from Source is greater than need be. Take the time to remove the thoughts and beliefs that hinder you or attract situations you don't necessarily want and begin your journey back to Source. Becoming one with Source is everyone's goal. It is the ultimate goal, whether you are aware of this fact, or not.

Can you imagine what the world would be like tomorrow morning, if everyone woke up and had eliminated all their fears and traded self-doubt for deeply loving themselves and their Source? This type of true acceptance of one's inner loving transformational power and increased connection to Source could eliminate all hate and war, overnight!

You have now been given an introduction into how this earth-plane existence functions and have been exposed to an introduction or explanation of the meaning of life. Make your next step a conscious step forward. When you have read this chapter, I know you are ready and I am proud of you for taking the first step! Now take another, you will be glad you did!

◈Chapter Thirty◈

How do I separate myself from being sad about the

seemingly horrible current disasters and current state of

human consciousness?

Lately, it appears as if there are increased amounts of disasters occurring around the globe. Economic failures, tsunami's, terrorism, volcanoes, earthquakes, hurricanes, tornadoes, political disputes, wars, shootings, the list goes on and on. Many of these happenings are man-induced, and natural forces cause many others. Most people would call these naturally created occurrences, "natural disasters." It is the negatively focused mind-set of many that call these happenings "natural disasters," rather than learning situations. Once you understand that thoughts are things, and we are all one, you begin to ask yourself the all important "WHY" question and learn from what happens around you.

When you are witness to a situation or occurrence, either directly or indirectly and have thoughts about it, you were also meant to have been part of its healing. Your awareness of a situation means you have been given an opportunity associated with the occurrence, to resolve something within yourself. We have options. We can focus on the seemingly negative occurrences, or conversely, deem them as learning opportunities and know they are not negative. Situations are opportunities, not occurrences to fear. A growing number of humans are currently adopting a fearless, loving, and non-judgmental mindset. They realize they are spiritual beings having a human experience and what happens, needs to happen until we all turn our thoughts to a more loving conclusion. They are beginning to understand the potential for each individual's positive input to the whole. Humans are noticing the potential for the collective consciousness and are being shown its healing possibility. The past several hundred years of mans ego-based treatment of Mother Earth has polluted the environment and taken advantage of her gifts. As mentioned before, everything must have balance. This holds true for Mother Earth, as well as for mankind. Currently, Earth is figuratively wagging its tail like a wet dog, due to what man has done as he creates the imbalances to nature. Mass cutting of our forests, the building of huge filthy cities, blacktopping the open fields with roads and cookie cutter housing developments, the dumping of toxic substances into our oceans, lakes and rivers and the rape of her natural resources, all for the sake of making a dollar, have all recently caused Mother Earth to attempt to cleanse herself. A hurricane might be a "Natural Disaster" for those who deem it so, or could also be considered an attempt by nature to clean up man's dirty work.

It is the human ego that says "I will do anything for power and generation of money, for I do not yet understand my connection to God." Jimmy Hendrix was a wild and creative person. Many people didn't respect his input because of his nonconformity, but listen to the truth found in his quote which went like this, "When the power of love overcomes the love of power, the world will know peace."

Am I negating the human suffering that has affected many by these natural occurrences? No, but rather than wallowing in victim mentality, I see these occurrences as signs and opportunity for change! Remember, it is our collective thoughts and actions, which contribute to the forces that have caused these occurrences

148

in the first place. I reiterate, these occurrences are an opportunity to take full responsibility for what you are witness to. Take a close look at where many of these so called "natural disasters" have taken place. Are these areas often over-populated, dirty, in need of a breath of fresh air? Compare these so called disaster areas to a clean unpolluted mountain brook, running through a pristine forest. Can you mentally see and feel the difference? Earth is reclaiming its original state and wants man to live harmoniously with her.

Wake up ego-based humanity! Waking up is exactly what is happening and it is beneficial to participate in this spiritual awakening. This shift in human consciousness is happening all around you, take a look for it and instead of judging it, ask what you can do to join in. Several decades ago it was uncommon for anyone in the USA to openly talk about this shift of human consciousness, spirituality or ability to connect with and know he is part of the God-force. Take a look back and locate how we were introduced to this shift, "Luke, use the Force" was a movie quote about something grander than most of us took it for. In 1983, Shirley MacLaine came out of the spiritual closet and proclaimed she was God in a book and movie made from the book called Out On A Limb. She took much ridicule and was the subject of jokes about her spiritual stance for many years until her words became more common knowledge. This is the dawning of the age of Aquarius, wasn't just a catchy song lyric from the play Hair. Movies such as Defending Your Life, Dragonfly, Dogma and What Dreams May Come are reflections of the current state of human consciousness and would have been inconceivable 50 years ago. Virtually any bookstore now has book after book about how to join in this mass awakening movement toward spirituality. It wasn't long ago when you had to search out a metaphysical or occult bookstore to find a book written by someone like Helena Blavatsky. Helena's esoteric words would tend to confuse and mystify compared to today's books, which are written in plain everyday language. Today one doesn't have to travel to London and seek out Watkins Books (the oldest Metaphysical bookstore in the world) to find a work on spirituality and self-discovery. Oprah wasn't given the opportunity to become a household name just to help locate a sad souls real father after a DNA test. There are other tabloid talk shows to handle that task! She has used her influence to introduce to the world the works of Eckhart Tolle, one of the most influential spiritual authors and teachers of our time! Oprah's' show called "Super Soul Sunday" has given us the opportunity to be introduced to the loving teachings of some of the greatest spiritual leaders of our time and simultaneously be witness to the spiritual awakening we all have access to.

This current reawakening of humanity and connection to Source, sometimes referred to as the "spiritual revolution," has also caused a need for balance. When we are witness to mass shootings and thousands killed by tsunamis, we are seeing the opportunity for balance to consciously join our loving energy together to add positive thought to the universe. Concentrate and focus on the good that happens in the world. Heal yourself from within. Don't wait for peace to come to the world. That may be a long way off. First find peace within yourself.

An individual can contribute to the momentum of the creation of world peace by being grateful and seeing the beauty in everything regardless of what people say on the news. Someday when more of us make the shift toward trusting in the almighty positive force and choosing loving thought over doom and gloom, the television and newspaper news, which constantly bombards us with negative, censored words, will have a smaller audience. When there is a smaller audience tuning into food for a souls pain (news), because there is no pain, the negative news will go out of business. They will have to close their newsroom doors, or alternatively choose to bring us the positive news.

As peace grows collectively we will see an increase in the acceptance of any human color, any faith, any sexual preference and any belief. Human kind will begin to see the beauty in all that unfolds and will treat Mother Earth with respect. Fossil fuels will cease to be used and renewable energy sources will continue to replace them. Social entrepreneurship will keep growing and human starvation will slowly become a thing of the past. These and even better wonders will continue to flourish as more people begin to heal as they expand their spirituality and connection to Source. OR, conversely, mankind will cease to exist and will have to start all over.

DO OVER?
It is quite possible.
It's possible that a do over has taken place in the past!

❧Chapter Thirty-One❧
What is victim consciousness and
how do I find out if I am stuck within it?

Our emotions are energy signposts to help determine our current state of negative or positive thought pattern. Anything that makes you feel unrest or a lack of inner peace is a wake up call to heal, ask why, and work upon yourself to change thoughts of fear to thoughts of love. I am well aware of the fact it is very easy to say those words, but conversely often difficult to accomplish. But I can guarantee a reduction in the content of your negative mental baggage will present you with freedoms, and offer a step up on the virtual ladder toward inner peace. Your vibration will increase and what will be attracted to you will be deemed an improvement over your past. It is up to each individual to find the courage, fortitude and resultant empowerment in themselves and begin to take an active part in making a shift towards the positive.

Victim consciousness requires that you need someone's assistance to make things right. There are always the negative mind-sets of judgment and blame involved in being a victim. Victimization is the state of mind that says to you, woe is me, this shouldn't happen to me, this is unfair, someone should pay for how I feel, HELP! It is alright to get help, but know that the goal is to be totally responsible for what you are witness to and that a balanced emotional state with a connection to God will allow you to go through and beyond your sometimes unwanted, attracted learning opportunities. Quite often it is the difficult, painful, learning opportunities that are a sign that true awakening is around the corner. When your negative generated thoughts are replaced

152

by loving thoughts, your life becomes easier. Let go and let God, is a mental place to strive for. Let it become a game within your mind to identify negative thought as you ask yourself "what am I supposed to learn from this situation, or why have a attracted this, and why do I feel uneasy?" Identify the thoughts that are not in your best interest, such as thoughts of judgment toward another and see how you can raise your energy level, as you replace them with a more loving approach. After such a mental exercise, ask yourself, "do I feel free, lighter or maybe even a tad happier, since I stopped judging"? If not, there is an internal mental trait or meme that needs to be found, changed and healed.

Identifying, challenging and changing the thoughts that do not serve you well, are the first steps toward inner peace. When you do so, give yourself a pat on the back. Congratulate yourself! Inner peace is a lack of negative thought or worries and instead a willing mental habit of creating happiness within, takes their place.

It is being committed to expanding the souls energy by living in the now and eliminating any possible angst within the mind that helps you walk toward inner peace. Conversely, when you consciously or subconsciously accept that you are a victim, you have decided to stay in a negative, painful, mindset.

ᰔChapter Thirty-Twoᰕ
I am still confused, what exactly is the EGO?

The masses usually describe the ego as a controlling narcissistic self-opinion that one has about himself. Quite possibly a grander self image than what the world sees. But it can also be seen as the false self. This false ego-based opinion about who you are, is based on what possessions you have, who you know, or what you do. It is the ego, which is responsible for generating thoughts of blame and judgment in an authoritarian attempt to be right. The false-self or ego loves to feel better about itself and will often not stop at any action that attempts to fill the whole that a lack of personal acceptance and connection to Source could offer. The ego enjoys its hold over your conscious and sub-conscious mind by offering and feeding on painful thoughts. The ego adopts all the teachings since birth (truths or lies) and will often compensate within the mind to cope with the pain of uncomfortable learned memes. The ego <u>loves</u> drama. The ego will attempt to control one's mind by reliving the painful past or offer up emotional outbursts of judgmental righteousness. When you want retaliation for what you have concluded was an unfair happening, you can be sure you are being controlled by your ego. Spiritual teachers will recommend that you love and accept the ego, and in your mind, shrink the ego down to a small size, place it in your heart, forgive it and mentally communicate to the ego that you are now in control, as you choose to take a more loving mental attitude. The peaceful emotions that you can generate from such an action are signposts that you are healing and walking toward inner peace. Don't wait for peace to come to the world, find peace from within! If negative emotions continue and are still controlling your state of mind after confronting the ego, it is recommended that you re-consult Chapters 4, 11 and 22 of this manual.

Here are some examples to help you identify ego-based actions and thoughts. When one hits a home run in a major league baseball game, the ego thinks that is a grand happening. A happening that says to oneself, "look at me, I am better then you, I hit a home run"! Another example might be a stockbroker who has accumulated wealth by personally creating nothing, but drives around in an expensive car in hopes all others will see him and think he is better then everyone that drives a less expensive car. Another would be a womanizer who feels better about himself after he takes advantage of a woman, sexually. I am not saying that the above three examples cannot happen with non-ego positive intention. I am saying that when these actions are created for a false sense of accomplishment, often at the expense of another, the ego is involved.

Having possessions and making accomplishments are not evil but pumping up a personal false sense of who you are, based on them, is a detrimental hindering mindset to finding your true-self. Your true self is the timeless energy and accumulated wisdom of your soul. One, who challenges the ego or false self, normally gradually adopts a humble but powerful connection to Source and is on the path to finding his true self.

Life's challenges can begin to reveal a journey toward becoming one with God. Often one will experience an almost overwhelming power of love, once the ego-based self is challenged, and walls surrounding the heart begin to break down. Your true self is the part of you that is connected to Source, God, Allah, Buddha, the Tao and all other things. Your true-self never dies, it is eternal, but your false-self or ego-based physical body, will. It's inevitable. You enter this world without possessions and you will leave this world without possessions. But your true essence or soul never dies. Dr. Wayne Dyer had said, when you have nurtured the false sense of who you are, you have "Edged God Out", the acronym for the EGO.

As you begin to connect with Source you begin to discard the egos need to be right. You understand everyone has the right to his or her own journey and self-discovery. You accept others for they too are a part of God. It can offer a revelation to the Authoritarian ego based mindset when asked, do you want to be happy or do you want to be right? This question challenges the ego-based mind and offers a healing alternative.

One on a spiritual path who has begun to understand the ego, begins to realize their achievements are not who they really are, nor do they give oneself true power. Only as you nurture the true self by realizing you are part of the Force do you begin to understand your true power. As you offer love to others you simultaneously offer love to yourself! Observations such as these must be softly understood and internalized in a way that circumvents the false self.

If the false self wants to feel grander or better than another because of a spiritual discovery and his connection to God, he has missed an opportunity to shed his false-ego. He has failed to understand the bliss of what his true connection to Source can offer.

⚜Chapter Thirty-Three⚜
How do I recognize and challenge my ego?

Recognize the ego by watching for the internal controlling essence that says you are better then someone else. Ego needs to surround itself with grand illusions derived from possessions, accomplishments, being right, being judgmental, perfectionism, opinions and name dropping. The ego can also feed you negative thoughts as it attempts to keep you in mental pain, such as reminding you of a regretful past. When you realize your true self-value exits by realizing the fact that you are part of the Force or God, you have challenged the false self. By doing so, you have lessened the ego's control over your thoughts and actions. It is helpful to mentally separate from the egoic mind and observe its control. You then have a choice to limit it's power over your internal mental make up. By seeing the ego as separate from your true self, decisions over it's ability to control your thoughts can be made. Becoming a watcher of your ego allows you to observe how the ego has control over your thoughts. As you watch, you now have the power to change what gives you mental anguish by replacing positive thoughts where need be.

It can be helpful to contemplate the Earth's smallness in comparison to the infinite universe and nurture the feeling of humbleness. Humble is a trait the ego will resist. Begin by asking yourself why you act in a certain way, especially when it is a knee jerk automatic response to someone, or to a negatively perceived situation. Examine if you were motivated to act from the egos need to intentionally hurt, belittle another, feel superior, feel smarter, feel right, more clever, better looking or any other selfish way of the ego. Now attempt to search for an optional way to act the next time that same situation or thought arises. Devise a way to act that makes you feel better by being kinder, more loving, more forgiving or with more understanding.

Knee jerk reactions to something perceived as an "outside of yourself" emotional difficulty, is always a reflection of what needs to be healed within yourself. It is an opportunity to find what needs to be healed by using honest introspection and look for and pray for a personal healing. You will be surprised how the external difficulty will no longer exist in your reality, when a true internal healing takes place! Ask, "does this new way of acting seem right but feel difficult to do because the ego's hold is too strong?" Does judging another fulfill your emotions? You can identify the ego because it loves emotional imbalance.

Discovering and admitting an emotional imbalance exists, means you are becoming aware of the painful place the ego resides. It can be helpful to identify the traits of the ego by understanding you are a pawn in the many advertising agencies ads, which manipulate and sell products by implications that feed the ego. Exposure to and belief in such chicanery, helps feed the false self image. Advertising is often created to control your ego by attempting to create its unattainable image. The ego is the part of the mind that get's excited about a soon to be new purchase that was conceived after being controlled by advertising. If you are susceptible to compulsive purchases and you want to stop, you might have to force yourself to wait a few days after your decision to make a purchase. After the cooling off period ask your self if you truly need what you were going to buy, or was it just going to make you feel better than another or to be a happier person. Purchasing happiness often occurs to make the false self briefly satiated and you will be doomed to go through the compulsive buying process, over and over.

It is important to know that when challenged, the ego will strongly retaliate. You gain power over the ego when you can observe its retaliation and choose a different response. An example of an egoic retaliation could happen after you experience a difficult minor road rage from another driver. Your thought system may have rationalized that retaliatory anger toward another

158

is only going to make you upset. You may have internally said, "that other person is just having a bad day, I will let this incident go." If you have an internal anger issue, whether you are aware of it or not, the ego might step up to the front of your mind. The ego doesn't want to be wrong and wants your anger to surface. What often is the case is a mental picture or thought arises that will attempt to make that other driver wrong, imbalanced, mean, and deserving of a verbal tongue lashing or the recipient of a particular finger gesture! The ego loves to make us miserable and will re-run these situations in our mind, over and over until we get beyond the internal need to balance our negative memes. An experiment to prove the ego's hold over you could involve the next time you judge another driver who was deemed by you to be driving badly. Ask yourself, did that other driver act that way due to having a health issue, minor heart attack or was he possibly rushed and heading to the hospital for assistance? Hmmm. This new look at another's actions produces more inner peace, no?

A physical way to challenge the ego's hold on oneself and identify it is to greatly alter your habits. The ego loves sameness, so you will begin to challenge the egos hold over you when you make changes in your normal routine. When you change your diet, pray to a higher power for help in diminishing the egos hold over your thoughts, wake up early and meditate, or alter your exercise routine you are challenging the ego. These are but a few of the actions that can help you to soften your ego's hold on you. Anything to make the ego confused is a great way to lessen its influence over you. Further identify the ego and how strong it is by observing the egos rationalizations as to why you won't be able to follow through with the challenges you have chosen, to expose its strength.

By saying "no" to the ego you will be taking a step toward inner peace. Remember that each step toward inner peace is a gift to not only you, but to everything and everyone else. You will be taking part in raising the level of human consciousness, which is a very worthy reason for living.

Love the ego, metaphorically diminish the ego and place him to sleep in a small place in your heart. Your ego need not dominate your life. The ego is often coupled with the energy of the wounded child within that may have been less than nurtured and loved, as it grew older. It may be necessary to love the inner child and treat it the same way as I suggested for the ego. Love the inner child, be it's new loving parent and metaphorically place it in a safe spot in your heart. Become the nurturing parent to that wounded internal little child within. If deemed necessary, re-read Chapter Four and consult John Bradshaw's book on re-parenting.

Some of these actions to help diminish the ego can be difficult to achieve until you balance out emotions that are stuffed and buried in your mind. Emotions are just energies that want to be expressed and released. This release sometimes requires help from external guidance (life coach, therapist, willing friend, etc.) due to the strength of the emotions. Emotions and fears, to balance out, need to be allowed room to be present and grow to their full extent. In your mind, safely allow them to be seen and accepted. If you need to physically act out the emotion, depending on which one it is, with a good cry or by hitting a pillow, allow that to happen. Since emotions are energy, when they are allowed some freedom, rather then being stifled, they will begin to dissipate. Outside guidance can help by offering a safe place and method of emotional release. If you are a person who is unable to show emotion in front of others, it is acceptable to be alone when attempting to release negative emotions but be aware that if the release is uncontrollable, you should seek professional help immediately. Seek help with a therapist or life coach if you are afraid of the emotions intensity or if you have difficulty identifying it. Just know that you are not your negative emotions, they are energies that can be eliminated when identified and allowed the space to move. Burying the emotions internally in time will be detrimental to your physical and mental well being. Let them move through you and eliminate them from your true self. To find out more about the thoughts and emotions that don't endorse you, read David Burn's book called <u>Feeling Good - The New Mood Therapy</u>. David's info is in the reference section. If you are skilled at honest introspection, watching J. P. Sears YouTubes can be an inexpensive and valid way to help yourself. He offers both humorous and nicely presented videos concerning physcology. **#21**

❧Chapter Thirty-Four❧
Who were the Hunas?

In the past there were many ancient but wise cultures that existed on our planet. The Hunas were one of those spiritually advanced cultures that lived in and around the Hawaiian Islands. You may be familiar with the term, The Big Kahuna. That was a reference to the Huna culture. The Hunas had a wonderful three part philosophy that stated;
Live in the Present
Trust Yourself &
Expect the Best.
When you can follow these three traits by living your life under their precepts, you are following in the positive attributes of a Huna inspired life. Attempt to discard any intention, action or thought that doesn't fit into one of those three categories.
Interested in the Huna way? Serge King's book about the Hunas is called <u>Huna: Ancient Hawaiian Secrets for Modern Living</u>.

◄§Chapter Thirty-Five§►
Can I become aware of the potential
for positive personal change?

Yes. By noticing what you attract into your life you are becoming conscious. Stepping to the side, in your mind, and observing your thoughts, has great power over the automatic thought process that the ego uses to control you. You are not those thoughts; so separate from them, observe them. Personal power is found when you consciously choose thoughts that will be in your best interest and replace the ones that are not. You can literally watch for those uncomfortable emotions that surface during a seemingly negative experience and allow them room to surface. Deal with those emotions and let them dissipate. They are energy and will dissolve when treated this way. Continue to be the watcher of your thoughts. If those negative thoughts arise again, stop them by being the watcher of your thoughts and by eliminating knee jerk reactions. Once again, give that emotion room to grow and dissolve. This process may take several times based on the severity and depth of your judgmental, emotionally charged, negative thought system. As you begin to heal those often early childhood learned beliefs and reactions that make you uncomfortable, you take a step toward inner peace. It is an allowing of those thoughts to control you and a resistance to change that keeps you in an unwanted circular learning processes pattern that never ends.

A recommended tool for changing an identified trait within the mind is the book called <u>Breaking The Habit of Being Yourself</u> by Dr. Joe Dispenza. He also offers a two part meditation CD, which guides you to alternative perceptions as he helps you to release old unwanted mental traits called <u>Body Parts</u>

In Space.

Begin to be thankful for those past seemingly negative experiences for their intention was to offer you freedoms through potential growth. Shed the unwanted uncomfortable experience and leave the past behind by seeking help and experiencing forgiveness. Noticing all experiences as a reflection of what the internal you has created, will allow you to change your level of consciousness by dropping negative thoughts, such as blame, and therefore allow you to change your reaction to what you attracted.

Use the mirror system to make internal personal changes and your world will change in direct proportion to the different vibrations emanating from the new thoughts. The mirror system is when you recognize in others, a kind or bothersome trait and at the same time understand what you are actually seeing is a reflection of what is inside of you. This is the beauty of the mirror system, as it reflects the internal you, as seen in our relationships with others. Without being honest about the mirror system, we slow our journey toward enlightenment for we tend to adopt blame and judgment as it's alternative. It is also a wonderful way to understand that you are responsible for absolutely everything that you experience. Your state of being, the people in your life, your health, even the dependability of the machines that you own, exists as a direct result of your conscious and subconscious thoughts. You might not have caused that fender bender in your car the other day, but your energy was a match to the one who was involved in the accident with you. Thoughts that arise from anger, blame, insecurity, guilt, shame, and selfishness are all ego-generated thoughts that can be changed by healing the inner you. Your thoughts do create your reality. To learn more about the mirror system, read Shakti Gawain's book called Living In The Light and to prove that your thoughts are creating your reality, see the Hay House book called E-Squared: Nine Do-It-Yourself Energy Experiments That Prove Your Thoughts Create Your Reality by Pam Grout.

When you ask for something or pray, that is your way of talking to the powers that be, your guides or Source. When you meditate and quiet the mind, you will begin to hear communication talking back at you from the powers that be, your

163

guides or Source. Don't be afraid to ask questions before you meditate or go to sleep. Answers often will just show up in your physical world, dreams or in your mind. Watch for the answers and when they show up, thank Source for the help. Being grateful strengthens the connection!

❦Chapter Thirty-Six❧
What does it mean to live in the "NOW"?

One of the greatest spiritual teachers of our time is Eckhart Tolle. Eckhart explains in his book, The Power Of Now, the importance of being a watcher of your thoughts. As you become a watcher of your thoughts, you become aware of the ego's need to be grand, in the limelight, selfish, self-centered and thoughts about why you need to change. This awareness allows you to see how the constant chatter of your internal thought process is running your life.

As you step to the side and observe this thought process, you begin to access the real you: the inner part of your essence that is eternal and connected to the all loving Source. The logical next step is to challenge those controlling thoughts and lovingly begin to replace the thoughts that don't serve you well. In a non-chastising way, begin changing the thoughts that belittle your true self by eliminating the egos need to be better than another. Your true self-value arises out of connection to the eternal Source, not by belittling or being better than another to feed the false ego self.

After the lessening of those constant ego-based thoughts, you can practice what Eckhart calls "living in the now." What does "living in the now" entail? "Living in the now" is a state of being. It is beyond normal thought or closer to an absence of it. It is an experience rather than a thought about the experience. You cannot be in the grip of the ego while living in the now, for you are fully experiencing the present moment. Living in the now includes an acceptance of what is. Living in the now is an attempt to touch the divine while still being awake. Up until recently this was possible only in meditation. By living in the present moment and finding the true bliss that is always present in the now, you have eliminated the regrets of the past, and the worry about the future. When living in the now you are not in the grips of thought but in a blissful state that can be likened to the state a talented musician or artist might be in, when fully engrossed in the creative process. This is sometimes referred to as being "in the zone." Living in the now is being present and being in that zone. Thought has stopped; true connection to Source has taken over. One sometimes isn't even aware of how beautiful the now can be until he once again, slips back into the more familiar ego-based thoughts concerning the need for change, the past or the future. When that happens, one then observes how wonderful being in the "now place," truly was.

Meditation is also a great place to begin to access "the zone," the now, or this lack of thought and connection to Source. The catch 22 of the meditative process is that after one decides to meditate, thoughts must be stopped to successfully meditate. One must access the zone of non-thought to let the "now" experience begin. You see, thinking and meditating are total opposite places within the mind and both cannot be experienced at the same time. Therefore, after determining you want to meditate by thinking you would like to do so, you will actually have to let go of any thought, to meditate successfully.

◈ Chapter Thirty -Seven ◈
What is the circular theory of thought?

To explain this theory I must first start with observations which I am sure you have been witness to. Look around the universe and attempt to determine the perfect shape. Observe that it is the circle which matter likes to be shaped into by natural forces. You can observe it in a drop of water, the shape of the sun, moon and countless other things. It is natural to be in a circle. When you apply that circular shape to the thought process you will begin to observe how thoughts begin, where they lead, and where they will end up, based on their initial intention. Initial intentions are the important two words in that last sentence. If you only take one concept with you from this chapter, take this one. The intention part of your thinking will lead you to a similar conclusion. Example: let's say you are in need of money because you are currently unable to attract financial abundance into your life. Your thoughts are constantly thinking, "I don't have enough, I have to get more, I can't ever make enough money to pay the bills. I feel helpless when it comes to attracting and holding onto large sums of money." What your mind is saying is you are locked into a strong belief system about the lack of ability to provide, you're not worthy and you believe in a frustrating system of lack. These are called memes. A meme is a learned mental thought that you have put credence in and have decided to believe. Your reaction might be to set out to attract money into your life. You decide to say abundance affirmations, start to visualize money in your pockets, you work hard and start a small business and take out advertising to get people to trust you enough to give you money. What happens when you begin an action started from a thought pattern of "I don't have enough", is that the forces that be, only recognize, the "I don't have enough," original intention of your thought. So the forces that be will keep the free flow of money from easily coming into your life. If you can reverse your thoughts, beliefs and feelings about money and trust in the force to provide, you will be starting from a lack of fear and a trust in God. The result will be a shift in the ease of how money will arrive into your life. Observing this theory, to this catch 22 circle of thought, guides you to the realization that you go around the circle of thought and end up where you started.

Much of the content of this book is concerned with alternatives. Alternatives that through awareness give rise to change. That change can be within or to what exists in your immediate surroundings. As you unfold and become more aware of the contents of your mind, you will have to ascertain at what point you will accept who and what you are. With many, at the heart of all change, is unrest of what is. That unrest shows up as a need to change the thoughts that do not serve you well, your relationships, your finances, the place you live, your level of self love or maybe even the food you eat. Anything you want to change can mean you are doing battle with what you have deemed an unwanted situation or thought. If one examines the intention for any action or decision for change, one discovers that the underlying motivation is often dissatisfaction for what is. Don't get me wrong, I have found that change is not only necessary for growth but will happen regardless to your intention or choice for change. If you discover the driving forces behind your need for change has had the attachment of angstful dissatisfaction, you can explore optional intentions. If one decides to change due to unrest, one will change slowly as this approach will create more unrest along the way. As one gets to a point of accepting what is and who they are, peacefulness sets in. A shift in the intention from one of dissatisfaction to one of giving takes place when acceptance of what is occurs. This shift can offer up a wonderful freeing metal state of mind.

Examining the need for change with the circular theory of thought one begins to see that change can be a battle or an easy peaceful accepting, based on the motivating forces behind the original intention.

If one is unhappy and attempts change due to being unhappy, one has consciously or unconsciously made the decision to make changes the difficult, angstful and slow way of doing so. Ester Hick's would describe that method as paddling upstream. **#22** It's harder to paddle upstream then it is to turn around and go with the flow. True happiness is feeling good about yourself and who you are. It includes a positive inner self-value system. One who doesn't have true inner happiness will most likely attempt to find happiness outside of themselves. This search for external happiness leads to addictions. Addictions can be anything from alcohol to being obsessed with how many LIKES one gets on a Facebook post. False happiness is when you feel happy only about external happenings such as compliments from other people, applause, and feeling value from what you do. If you are unhappy, ask yourself what is blocking your true inner happiness from existing. There may be an emotional trauma or wounded inner child that is inside your subconscious mind that needs healing through introspection and finding what your gifts are to the world. Once again, we can see that proof of truth is discovered on the inside. By watching internal thoughts and determining the intention behind life's decisions, one becomes aware of whether they have decided to paddle upstream or not.

Your dominant conscious and sub-conscious thoughts,

beliefs and feelings are what need to change when you are not manifesting your desires. You can say "I trust" thousands of times, but if your feelings are stuck in a meme, fear, or an internal belief when defining your current state of reality, your actions will have difficulty arriving at your chosen result. Dr. Wayne Dyer would ask, "if you choose to think the thought that believes you are not worthy of financial abundance, you are accepting a learned meme about yourself, which may or may not be true." Now ask yourself "what is the exact opposite of that thought" and align yourself to Source when the answer arrives. The exact opposite, which may or may not be true, would be that you are worthy of financial abundance. Since anything is possible when Source is the driving force behind your thoughts, why would you choose the first limiting thought instead of the second thought? Thoughts are vibration, thoughts create your reality so by aligning with the thought that you are worthy of financial abundance, you are willing to allow financial abundance, and for the moment that you have financial abundance, you have started your circular theory of thought from a positive place. Along with this new thought concerning abundance, banish the doubt. Search inside for the feeling you would emanate, knowing you are wealthy. Replace the old fear of lack feelings with the new secure, wealthy feeling. When you can accomplish this new shift in consciousness a new, positive, wealth vibration has been created.

By not focusing on lack, you have been given the gift of possible positive outcome. If this makes sense to you, go within and ask yourself: how does it feel to think in this unlimited positive way? Does it feel freeing? Does it offer unlimited possibility? Has it reduced the power of that negative meme over your beliefs? After such questions and a true shift in intention, do you noticed a reduction in your fear of lack? A simple synopsis of this topic is, you end up in your reality, where you started from within your mind. Look within your mind, and be aware of where your thoughts started from, and what the intention was behind them.

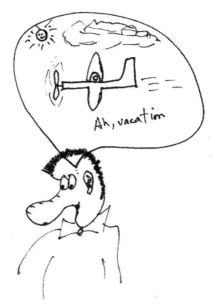

❧Chapter Thirty-Eight❧
How can visualization influence my reality?

Your mind is a powerful tool. What your current mental makeup is made of, (dominant thoughts, beliefs and feelings), is what determines what is attracted to you. Your mind creates your reality. Your mental makeup is created by your past experiences and chosen beliefs. Your mind cannot discern the difference between an experience and one that is visualized within your imagination. This is one reason Albert Einstein said "Imagination is more important than knowledge." As you visualize and use as many sensory perceptions as possible during that visual experience, your mind absorbs those feelings, smells, sights, sounds and pictures and sets out to bring that outcome into your reality. Thoughts are things, they are energy, and thoughts beget manifestation, so choose your thoughts wisely. For visualization to

171

be affective, intention is the key to creating a more loving place and positive karmic experience for yourself.

Michael Jordan used visualization and became the greatest basketball player in our history. You can use this tool as well. Shakti Gawain's book <u>Creative Visualization</u> is a good book to read as you begin learning how to visualize. Practice this tool and learn to see pictures in your mind. Some people who visualize, see what their desires are on an internally created mental movie screen and then their personally created mental film is played upon that screen. See it, feel it, smell it, get excited by what you are creating and banish the doubts! Positive emotion is a great ally to creating what you desire with your visualizations. When you start to visualize you have begun to dive into being a creator using visualization as a helpful tool. When you truly believe in your visualization you will feel a positive expectancy and excitement for your visualization's arrival.

Let it be known that if you have a partner in your spiritual journey, you can increase the power of your visualizations by visualizing together. You can further increase the power if you are a man and woman doing this visualizing together, as the opposite sexual polarity helps to complete the power of the visualization. Better still, 3 or more make the experience stronger yet! If you are new to the power of visualization, start manifesting small things and watch for the results. As mentioned before, you can start simply by closing your eyes and visualizing your desired parking spot at the mall. Banish the doubt and take that drive. As you improve your visualization skills you will see the wanted parking spots occur more frequently. This is a small but great step in giving credence to knowing and believing the power of your abilities. Knowing and believing are several of the first Laws of the Universe! If you could banish the doubt by flicking a switch, WOW THAT WOULD BE A POWERFUL TOOL!

If you attempt to visualize a negative occurrence, you will have difficulty with your desired outcome, not to mention that your karma will be directly involved. Keep this tool called visualization in your pocket but always accompany your sessions with "may this or something better be created for the greatest good on all concerned."

172

If you have trouble getting started with visualization try this experiment. Close your eyes, in your mind go to the refrigerator and take out a juicy, fresh, yellow lemon. Within your mind take a knife and slice off a piece of lemon on a cutting board, smell lemon, see the juice running onto the board, then squeeze the juice into a glass. Now add a little sugar, ice and water, stir. Did you begin to salivate? Did you see and possibly smell the lemon juice in your mind? If so, you are on your way to becoming an expert who visualizes and sees pictures in his mind.

❧Chapter Thirty-Nine❧

Life's Equation

$$\frac{\text{Guilt, Anger, Sadness, Judgment}}{\text{Fear}} \Bigg/ \frac{\text{Love}}{\text{Acceptance, Approval, Forgiveness}} = \text{Inner Peace}$$

or take the

shortcut &

Live In The Now

I am not a great mathematician; maybe this isn't quite clear to you, so let me try to explain;

Guilt, Anger, Sadness, Judgment, Acceptance, Approval, Forgiveness, regardless of whether they are positive or negative thoughts, are still thoughts. Thoughts are from the mind, which arise from beliefs and filters from our experiences that have occurred in the past. The past tells the mind what to think and how to react. For example, if you normally drive to the store and have arrived safely to the store each morning, you hold the thought that driving to the store is safe. One day you decide to walk to the store and on that day you get robbed. Your mind will now use this experience to create the thought/judgment that walking to the store is unsafe. However it turns out the person who robbed you was a drifter and was simply passing through town, which happens to be one of the safer towns in the country. Many people walk in town everyday and are safe. Based upon one past seemingly negative experience, the thought of being unsafe determines your future actions. A fear has been created by thought.

We can use the above portion of Life's Equation to work our way through this, and other experiences. Based on the event, you feel fear, anger, possibly even guilt if your mind is programmed to feel guilty. If you feel guilty your thoughts will have to move past these emotions. You will need to move to acceptance and forgiveness. Then on to the best one of all, love. Once you go through the above portion of the equation, you can gain inner peace.

How then can we move to the "live in the now" portion of the equation and utilize the shortcut to inner peace? It can be accomplished by living in the present moment. For example, you don't use hair clippers to eat with and do not carry them around with you. You only use the clippers when they are needed. Your mind is like the hair clippers. It is a tool. Use your mind when you need it. If you see a road closure sign up ahead, your mind will use its instincts to tell you to stop and find another route. You don't need to use your mind to think about what happened to you the year before, when you may have felt horrible. Thinking about what made you feel horrible in the past at that moment can only generate more negative thought. Since thought is energy those past negative thoughts will cause your energy to fluctuate up and down based on their content.

This is similar to watching a beautiful aria being sung by the most perfect opera singer in the world and instead of looking directly at her, you record the performance on your cell phone. Then you proceed to watch the performance on your phone video recording. You have totally missed the "now" moment. One excuse used to avoid not living in the present moment is "but I feel guilty in the present moment." If this is the excuse then this person is not living in the present moment, they are still utilizing past thought to dictate what they place their attention on. By focusing on what is happening at this very moment (the now), you push away past and future thought from your mind.

By choosing to use the "living in the now" shortcut, you start to focus on the now. You begin to experience "life" rather then reliving the past or attempting to forecast your future experiences.

It has been proven that the mind cannot multitask and have two conscious thoughts simultaneously. Therefore, if you focus your attention on what is happening to you at this very moment, you will, at least for the time you focus on the now, find it impossible to feel guilty, angry, seek approval or the need to forgive. All of that will be gone and in your mind you will begin to flow downstream, instead of fighting your thoughts in an up stream manner. To prove this, the next time you observe and catch yourself thinking a negative thought, stop and concentrate on your breath, take several slow deep breaths. Next concentrate on your hands, by observing the feeling in them. Now observe something to find beauty in. Look for something you can appreciate which is right in front of you. It could be a bird in flight or the wind moving the leaves of a tree. After this experiment, become the observer of your current thoughts to look for dissipation in the level of the original negative thought. If you were successful with following the above directions you will conclude that the "now" is a less stressful place then its negative options.

With practice this process can take you to a level of inner peace without all the emotional angst! You see there are only two types of emotions. Some feel good and some feel bad. All good feeling emotion is sourced from thoughts originating from a loving perspective. Living in the "now" eliminates the bad, as the mind cannot find it.

⋞Chapter Forty⋟
Where is mankind headed?

Man is currently moving through a large transition. Everyday, more people become aware of the spiritual progress that is awakening all over the planet. That awareness and the opposite of that awareness are what are pulling the forces that be, in seemingly opposing directions. Predominantly, where man is overcrowding and ignoring Mother Earth and or polluting, she is wagging her tail, so to speak. Let's attempt to cleanse the Earth she is saying, when she causes an earthquake here, a devastating hurricane there, not to mention the tsunamis', volcanoes, flooding, nuclear disasters, typhoons, dust storms and droughts, to name a few. You have noticed a rise is the quantity of those occurrences, haven't you? As those occurrences continue to happen and 100's of thousands lose their lives, the Earth breathes a tad lighter as she continues to cleanse. After seemingly negative occurrences, the weak often become more fearful and from an energy standpoint contribute to future disasters. Conversely, the enlightened walk forward without fear, as they know they will never die but merely change in form. If mankind awakens too slowly, there is a good chance they will annihilate themselves. It has probably happened before and it could happen again. Time is of no consequence to Source and God has no time clock. This is why it is so important right now that you open yourself up to your spiritual growth, take an active part in cleansing the Earth, and rise above the petty everyday things humans commonly focus on.

177

Proof of early man has recently been discovered and is called Australopithicus Africanus. This early version of humanoid lived somewhere between 2.5 and 3 million years ago. Early man's focus was on food. He later found the use of tools and sought shelter. So lets take a look at the needs of early primitive man. He spent all his time gathering food, hunting animals, procreation and sought out shelter. Modern man on the other hand needs food, loves to procreate with other humans and builds shelters. Maybe we are not as advanced as our ego's like to think. Three million years have gone by and we are basically doing the same things. My vision of this early time goes a little like this. It was a fine day that UUGGG (the name I give to our primitive hunter) killed that small animal to eat, had a full belly and rested next to a large tree. He was unaware of the storm that headed his way, as his stomach was full and he was sleeping very deeply. He awoke with a start when the lightning struck and threw his body 20 feet away from the now burning tree and didn't even notice the remains of his kill until the flame died down and his first BBQ was noticed. As his headache subsided, he tasted the cooked animal. UUGGG liked it. He tasted it for three days after that, he still liked it and the food didn't get rancid as fast as the raw meat he was accustomed to eating. UUGGG still didn't have the capacity to think very deeply, he just noticed that his food was better cooked. It didn't spoil as fast and he began to have free time due to the cooking of meat that was now part of his weekly regime. He had time to make better tools, keep the fire going and improved his shelter. He had time to chase after his buddy's female companion and all seemed well. What then after his basic needs were met did UUUGG do with his spare time? I offer the theory that being part of God's creation he turned to the creation of art. He was expressing himself by shaping sculptures out of mud and using pigments to draw on the cave walls. His instinct wasn't the gathering of more material possessions it was to create! He was emulating his creator even though he was unaware of who that might have been. He created for the mere fun, beauty and gratification it brought him. He wasn't going to trade his cave wall to the highest bidder. It was merely a joy to create or had spiritual significance. Philosophy and thought were in the future. Looking at today's human

178

consciousness I observe that we have an easier life then UUGG. We have better tools, abundant food sources, instant fire, more comfortable shelter and many a possible willing mate. We read, communicate, think, have more free time, but our consciousness has not evolved side by side with our inventiveness and the information which we rely on. We are rudimentarily very similar!

Most people are focused on daily concerns about food, water, money, possessions, relationships etc. and are unaware that by increasing their spirituality and losing some negative thoughts, those daily concerns dwindle in importance. They can begin to feel fulfilled due to their vibrations having increased in frequency and what they need begins to show up in their lives. Creativity becomes paramount.

As more people rise above their fears and doubtful self loathing, they give a boost of vibrational energy to not only God but to everyone else. It can become your gift to the Universe and will help with the loving transition that is occurring at this time in man's evolution.

Let's consider that man awakens to walk with self love, without fear and with God. In a resulting Utopian Universe, I surmise that we would eventually abolish many of the controlling aspects of government or abolish government entirely, as there would be no need for Capitalism, Communism, Socialism, Totalitarianism or any "ism" for that matter. Nor would we have a need for things such as welfare, wars, laws, money, or taxes. To give you an example of how one of the "ism's" is not spiritually oriented is to describe what Capitalism is driven by. In a Universe where karmic results of actions and intentions determine future experience, how can a Capitalistic society last indefinitely? It most likely cannot. Capitalism's main drive is to have a product or service and then ask another for more than it is worth. Capitalism is profit oriented. Human nature as it exists now leans toward taking advantage of that system, making more money then they could ever need due to the fear of lack. Therefore distribution of wealth is greatly unbalanced. In an intelligent system that says, "as you giveth, so shall you receive", Capitalism doesn't fit neatly into that scenario. Compare that concept with a similar test where an uneducated person attempts to stuff a square block into the circular hole. It just doesn't work very well. In this imagined Utopian society, man would be totally aware of karma and give freely to his fellow man. He would know that as he gives, so shall he receive. His creativity would create things, ideas, food, or whatever he was good at creating and then share his talents or products with anyone who would be interested in receiving them. The main attribute of creation would evolve into the joy of process, rather than attempting to intentionally profit from it. He would also understand that whatever he might want would be out there for his asking. There would be no need of money, no striving to beat another at anything for when everyone loved themselves, there would be no need to be better than another. Equality would finally, lovingly exist. There would be enough to go around, food, shelter, and sustainable natural energy etc. The lack of fear of death, fear in general and judgment would eliminate all war, disputes and emotional imbalance would be a thought pattern of the past. Since everyone loves himself or herself and there were no limits when the God Force is part of ones makeup, they would teach those concepts to their children, therefore eliminating future humans need to fight for something they might consider scarce. Creativity would be a joyous, loving action and would be the driving force behind all sharing occurrences. This Utopian universe or something like it, will evolve in direct proportion to man's spiritual awakening. The latest news in early 2014 is that Switzerland is contemplating giving every adult a several thousand dollar a month wage for just being themselves. The thought behind this free wage is that their citizens would be in a much greater position to positively contribute to society. In other words someone in Switzerland is contemplating sharing the wealth to eliminate fear-based thought. This is an almost unbelievably positive step. Kudos to Switzerland! As of early 2016, groups are forming that are beginning to create a society based on philosophies similar to my Utopian dream. Such groups can be found on Facebook. One of these groups is called "Sustainable Human". You can enter those two words on the top of your Search Facebook window to find out more about them and how they are attempting to make these positive changes.

Now as individuals, let us all contribute to raising the level of human consciousness by taking conscious effort to change our thoughts from fear to love, in order for the world to reflect back the beauty that could exist. Let us continue to evolve, and help erode away the wars, jealousies, hate and deceit that arise from profit-oriented, non-spiritually inclined ego-based business, politics and humanity.

I bid you peace and wish you success on your journey from fear to love!

⋘Chapter Forty-one⋙
Is there a mental state that would be in my best interest?

The mental state that would be in your best interest in order to become closer to the all loving Source, find inner peace and an absence of fear, is to choose to be happy and grateful! Happiness is an often overlooked state of mind. It can be elusive and even neglected. Most people confuse happiness with doing or receiving something they enjoy. Not true. Happiness is a conscious choice and is internally created separately from doing what you enjoy. Choose to be happy, give yourself permission to be happy and if you have to, fake it for 15 minutes until it begins to spread across your inner being, like frost on a winter window.

If you have difficulty creating, nurturing and keeping happiness in the forefront of your mind, find out how you can serve others. The act of service to others can be as simple as offering a genuine smile to a passerby, helping someone who has difficulty carrying their groceries to their car, to volunteering to help clean up a disaster site. Service, donation of time or physical offerings are the most universal ways to find out what true happiness really feels like. Also, being grateful for everything life has offered will allow wonderful energies to open up for you. The internal feeling of being grateful says to the Universe "All Is Well"!

As we discussed in the chapter on the circular theory of thought, you have to conclude that if you start at being grateful and happy, you will create more things to be grateful and happy about! The **intention** you start with is what you end up with. Just believe it and allow it!

May you be happy...

May you be well...

May you be peaceful!

"Conflict cannot survive
without your participation."
Dr. Wayne Dyer

Synopsis

Please surmise whether I have made spirituality clearer for you. I trust that I have helped you with a thought or two and I bid you peace.

Call this page a brief understandable statement for the meaning of life.

When you can remain in an all loving state of vulnerable total trust in The Force, while eliminating internal negativity, desire, judgment, control and the ego, you can then open yourself up to the elimination of all fear, by allowing fear to flow through you and dissipate. Deep down there are only two things that each of us really want. Those two desires are a want to be approved of and a need to be loved. A balanced approach to your mind, body and spirit are mandatory. All the false beliefs we were given and were adopted by us, allowed our ego to take advantage of us to compensate for the lack of those two basic desires.

Many a seeker will come to a point where his false self, inner demon, devil or ego has become unbearable. He may attract a situation that puts him in a less than worthy place. At that point, asking The Force for help, along with the act of surrender allows him to accept the existing negative thought energy to flow through and out. It is the only true healing option and there is no greater journey. Walking through the fear allows you to let it dissipate. When you eliminate fear, you can allow a shift toward being happy and grateful for everything that surrounds you, happens to you and that has happened to you. You say YES to life and what you attract to yourself. You lovingly allow happy acceptance of your current reality, as it is imperative to do so, and you begin to walk along with the peace of God in your pocket. You learn to live in the NOW. You are not flawed! You acknowledge you are a worthy part of The Force. It's that blissfully simple.

As you begin your spiritual journey, attempt to keep your thoughts introspective and simple. As most humans do, we tend to let our emotions run our lives. Learn to access the right side of your brain, as the left side can often complicate situations beyond our ability to endure. Life was not meant to be difficult. It is often our **reactions** to life, which make it into a struggle.

LOVE IS
ALL YOU NEED!

I bid you peace

Epilog

Every guide, self help book, or lecture attempting to sort out the meaning of life, should all end with a final chapter. This final chapter should be blank, for when we think we have the answers, it is at that precise moment that we discover we have only touched the beginning. For instance, as I write this I am starting to discover that we are in what I like to call a dream, a proving ground here on the Earth-plane, created by mass consciousness in which we choose, we discover, we grow and seek the ultimate goal of enlightenment by returning home to Source. Some call the earth physical experience an illusion. Somehow we were separated from God and the souls that are sent to have a human experience are learning to drop their fears and begin their journey back to connecting with God. This never ending cycle is why we learn and grow, while God grows.

Here on Earth we are experiencing one of many levels of the mind. We are not only all connected but collectively as a group we are responsible for all that we witness here on Earth. Fear thoughts are what I call Hell, and loving, forgiving thoughts are what can bring you Heaven on Earth. By living in the now and truly choosing only loving thoughts you can eliminate all thought that brings you pain. If you are in a judgment of another, you are in an ego-based fear-based reaction. One can ask Source for help to ease the pain you are putting yourself through. Remember that being humble can allow the magnanimous power of Source to work miracles in your life. Ask (pray) for the healing, allow it, step aside and stop attempting to control. When we try to control we are saying we are more powerful than God. Let Source bring to you the experiences and thoughts you need in order to heal your fear-based perceptions, which will begin to allow only the chosen loving thoughts to enter your mind. Is this an easy process? Not always, but you can be aware of the process and ask for help from Source.

As you begin to challenge the ego's hold on your mind, you will feel like a part of you is dying. The ego will lash out and grasp at thoughts of retaliation, but stay strong, choose loving forgiving thought and you will begin to step into the world of inner peace. Let this chosen transformation take its course. Be

187

kind to yourself and know you are your best coach. Don't rush, enjoy the ride, as the ride seemingly never ends. All your needs will be met based on your inner thought. It is possible to make the shift from fear to love without going through all the learning opportunities outlined in this manual, but I believe that an awareness of how the earth-plane existence functions is a great prerequisite to making the chosen transformation from fear to love, easier.

I have met well known famous spiritual lecturers and authors who were not aware of the fear-based thoughts they harbored. They talk of peace but yet are stuck in fear-based judgments and put up a fight against their deemed enemies.

As you become aware of the contents of your mind and learn how to begin your journey toward the transformation to loving thought, it is recommended to become familiar with a book called The Course In Miracles. By The Foundation For Inner Peace. Marianne Williamson has an interpretation of the Course that is a highly recommended starting point when you make your initial choice to shift to thoughts of love. Her book is called A Return To Love.

The importance of you making this shift is paramount at this point in time. Some aspects of consciousness are on a downward spiral and have the capability to annihilate mankind off the face of the Earth. This could happen if the collective fear-based thinkers stay more powerful than the rapidly growing new wave of people who are adopting a loving approach to self and personal empowerment. The world needs you to make your shift to loving thoughts in order to counteract the destructiveness of the fear-based mentality that exists. So creating peace within yourself really is more than just removing your pain, it truly is your saving and healing gift to the Universe. This process seems to be getting more difficult every week as the negative factions of humanity feel the pressure of the good. They will show their negative ways and love will help sway them from the darkness.

It has been said that if every person alive today woke up tomorrow with only unconditional love for all others and themselves in their hearts and had eliminated all thoughts of fear, the resulting world would instantly reflect a peaceful, harmonious,

188

war-free Earth. Such a shift in consciousness would create an Earth that would be based on a giving philosophy rather than a fear-based "gimme, gimme, make me safe" philosophy. Awareness of such makes each and every one of us an important part of the whole and once again brings to the forefront of our minds the concept that when we heal and love from within, we automatically project the positive energies created by doing so, to all others.

Everything we experience is merely a reflection of the contents of our mind (s). I have found that the use of meditation helps us remember the connection to Source and can guide us past the judgment of life's occurrences and others. Judgments will only bring us suffering. We can also ask for help before meditation to further end our suffering as Source can guide us past base emotions and baste us with a loving alternative.

Being aware of a trait or situation that you want to change is a worthwhile mental place to be. As you ask for help from the forces that be, concentrate on being one with the higher power. To find examples of how to word prayer (asking for help) for specific intentions, consult the works of Kyle Gray, Doreen Virtue and Marianne Williamson as found in the research tools at the back of this manual. Glean and bathe in Source's power, lack of judgment, unconditional love and inability to see anything as negative. Once you understand what the God-Force consists of, you will be able to concentrate on the positives rather than decide to do battle and fight against your negatives. Remember that as you resist, so shall it persist. Make a choice to be open to change, set the negative trait aside and concentrate on it's positive alternative. If you go within your mind to do battle against your unwanted traits, you often unconsciously give its existence credence. The unwanted trait becomes slower to transform or even strengthens, when you attempt to do battle with it. As you concentrate on the unwanted traits opposite, mentally walk forward, contemplate your chosen state, your new thoughts and especially how you feel as you mentally see yourself in the place where the new positive change exists.

Positive emotion surrounding the new you, plus the gratefulness and joy that accompanies such contemplation is a much stronger approach to positive change than doing battle

189

against it. After a prayer, watch for signs, synchronistic happenings, and random events that offer contemplation or alternatives to what might exist in your mind that would hinder or slow down the manifestation of the contents of your prayer. As mentioned before, you have to identify, give room to feel, and heal by releasing any fear that exists within your conscious or subconscious psyche that is not in alignment with your desires (prayers) for them to come to fruition. When answers arrive take note. Observe the freedoms, which are felt and found within. Big changes that have been washed with love often make one feel lighter. That lighter feeling is an increase in your vibration. As you give thanks for that positive step toward becoming one with the light (Source), let that feeling in, revelation and ah ha moments can become part of your daily life. Revel in them, bathe in it, create joyful emotions from it and give thanks again. When this happens for you, drop stagnant beliefs; the truths and connection to Source will take their place. Arriving at this point of awareness or awakening, can be truly grand. This awareness is felt in the heart chakra. A worthy part of the body to ascertain truths from!

Let in the loving alternatives and watch your life change for the better. Your thoughts are likened to the power of creation. Understand the importance of your thoughts and use them wisely. You are a creator!

As you shift in consciousness, be aware of how the world around you responds. You will be amazed at how this all works! Remember you are never alone. Be the observer of your mind and resultant reality. As you observe yourself, learn, grow, choose, listen and change. Learn to accept and be comfortable with who you are by joining the observer and who you are, by becoming one.

As you are witness to how the Universe works, you will understand the truth that your past has happened only to get you to the current moment in time. As you find understanding and wisdom in that, take it to the next step. That next step involves releasing the need to go any deeper into the healing of the mind. The past is no longer important as only the true bliss of connection to Source matters. You will simultaneously make peace with all that is, past included. Instant healing without the need for continued introspection takes place and living in the now will become a common happening. Beauty will begin to be found in everything. God's creation is astoundingly beautiful when you view it from this perspective.

When you accomplish this shift in consciousness, you will be free of the past and accept it as a loving occurrence. At this juncture, you will only be concerned with beauty, truth, love and the excitement of the almost unbelievable anticipation of what lies ahead, as God takes you to the next and the next and the next. The journey never ends so you can now look forward to that next.

All is well!

Note:

The author of this manual does not offer medical advice or prescribe the use of it's content as a treatment for medical issues. The information is offered as an adjunct to your positive well being and spiritual journey. The author assumes no responsibilities for your use of the material or your actions.

The concepts you have just read are gleaned from many sources. Some of them include the author, his wife Carol, his son Adam, his daughter Rebecca, spiritual guides, intuitive friends, the author's intuition, and the leaders in the spirituality educational field. David has studied with Dr. Wayne Dyer, Caroline Myss, and Stuart Wilde . He has had the pleasure of being in the presence of Mata Amrtanandamayi Devi and Louix Dor Dempriey. He has read, explored and applied the material found in the research tools section. Please find a list all the authors, spiritual teachers and books that have contributed to David's evolution and in many cases, this manual. If he has missed anyone, he apologizes. The author admits having had such an amazing life dedicating his existence to positive self-value growth, spiritual growth and heightened inner peace, it will be nearly impossible to remember everyone. David sincerely thanks you all. Please use the in-depth list of resources for further spiritual exploration, which will allow you to take a step closer to the never ending journey toward awakening and enlightenment. Let your heart direct you. Trust your intuition.

Your inner you will know which ones you will benefit from by reading first.

Start your spiritual DIET today!

<u>Daily spiritual smoothie recipe</u>

Take as needed for your spiritual health:

Blend any of these following ingredients,
as your loving perspective requires!

Say to yourself "I am what I am and what I am, is OK!"

Participate in an early morning 24 minute quiet time, meditation, positive reading or listening to a self help audio file. One minute for each ensuing hour of the day!

Daily, partake in a minimum of 20 minutes of yoga, Tai Chi, a brisk walk, or vigorous exercise of your choice.

Do something or say something nice to someone else with the intention of spreading love.

Create a Ten Most Wanted (Expected) List.
Read it aloud and write it down on paper daily.

Smoothie cont.

For 24 hours, until it becomes commonplace, Let 'GO" and let "GOD" or whatever Force you trust in. Remind yourself to do so frequently. Stop paddling up river! Cease resisting! Remove resentment, judgment, self pity, victim consciousness and go downstream. Do this until it becomes a daily habit. Live in the present, trust yourself and expect the best! Go with the flow while eliminating worry!

Participate in a guided audio chakra balancing until you can achieve it on your own.

Look into your eyes in the mirror and say to yourself:
    "I love and approve of myself"

Find something to be grateful for. Do this as often as possible!

Check if there is anyone, including yourself to forgive for anything. Practice taking responsibility for attracting that situation and then practice the art of forgiveness. Heal your inner child first, if necessary.

Visualize positive outcomes for the greatest good of all concerned.

Eat only alkaline foods for one day per week.
Alkaline foods are mainly certain nuts, certain grains, vegetables, most fruits, fruit juice without corn syrup or high fructose and organic leafy greens. For more info – Google "Alkaline Foods"

For deeper sleep:
Strange dreams are often the subconscious mind attempting to sort out and release the happenings of the day. Before going to sleep, take the day backwards in your mind. Find at minimum, five major activities from the present moment backwards toward the morning. You might drift into thought, but as you catch yourself, start this five-point reversal once again. This will help release the day and get you into REM sleep faster then usual.

References

Many of my references and research listings are links for your computer. Write the exact link into your browser to further research my sources or go to my website were hyperlinks will be accessible for your convenience.
www.newspiritualitydiet.com

1 - https://www.youtube.com/watch?v=Pwe-pA6TaZk
Or Google: "Matt Dancing Around the World 2012 YouTube"

2 - (http://reincarnation.nazirene.org/)

3 - https://www.britannica.com/event/Albigensian-Crusade can all help to put a different perspective on how religion has and is influencing man's development.
http://www.near-death.com/reincarnation/history/bible.html

4 - (http://abcnews.go.com/Nightline/video/joel-osteen-faith-positive-thinking-14524517)

5 - http://www.christianitytoday.com/ct/2012/april/defending-scripture-literally.html)

6 - (http://theskooloflife.com/wordpress/self-actualization-in-the-maslow-hierarchy/)

7   -
https://www.sciencedaily.com/releases/1998/02/980227055013.htm

8 - (http://www.alice-miller.com/en/preface-to-from-rage-to-courage/)

9   -   https://www.washingtonpost.com/news/answer-sheet/wp/2015/12/25/why-is-christmas-on-dec-25-a-brief-history-lesson-that-may-surprise-you/

10 - (http://www.dailygalaxy.com/my_weblog/2013/10/largest-structures-in-the-local-universe-reveal-an-unseen-mass-.html)

11 -(http://www.dailygalaxy.com/my_weblog/2013/10/largest-structures-in-the-local-universe-reveal-an-unseen-mass-.html)

12 - (http://www.goodreads.com/quotes/320376-the-beginning-of-freedom-is-the-realization-that-you-are)

13 - (http://www.livescience.com/25763-mayan-apocalypse_failure-believers-cope.html)

14 - https://en.wikipedia.org/wiki/Neotantra)

15 - http://www.amazon.com/Be-Healed-Earth-Warren-Grossman/dp/1583220194/ref=sr_1_1?s=books&ie=UTF8&qid=1455901109&sr=1-1&keywords=grossman+earth+healing

16 - http://www.amazon.com/Change-Your-Thoughts-Living-Wisdom/dp/140191750X.

17 - http://www.schwabfound.org/content/what-social-entrepreneur

18-
http://www.goodreads.com/author/quotes/2960.Wayne_W_Dyer?page=8)

19 -
http://www.ted.com/talks/louie_schwartzberg_nature_beauty_gratitude

20 - http://www.panachedesai.com/comments/free-content

21 - (https://www.youtube.com/watch?v=j67O34fMlHQ

22 - https://www.youtube.com/watch?v=HdRYP3OyKCo

Research tools for further spiritual growth and enjoyment Book, Tapes, Websites, CD's etc.

Books, meditations, lectures, DVD's by Dr. Wayne Dyer

"You Can Heal Your Life", the book and DVD by Louise Hay

"How To Love Yourself " Audio by Louise Hay - http://www.hayhouse.com/how-to-love-yourself-1

"Affirmations", "The Force", "Miracles" and all other works of the late Stuart Wilde

"Creative Visualization" and "The Four Levels Of Healing" by Shakti Gawain

"The Secret" By Rhonda Byrne

All the works of Jerry and Esther Hicks
"The Law of Attraction"
"Ask and It Is Given"

"E-Squared": Nine Do-It-Yourself Energy Experiments That Prove Your Thoughts Create Your Reality by Pam Grout

"Discovering Your Soul Signature" by Panache Desai

"The Complete Conversations With God" by Neal Donald Walsh

"Eat, Pray, Love" by Elizabeth Gilbert

"The Untethered Soul" by Michael Singer

"The Seekers Guide" and "Broken Open" by Elizabeth Lesser

"Breaking The Habit of Being Yourself" by Dr. Joe Dispenza
He also offers a two part meditation on CD or MP3 that guides you
to alternative perceptions as he helps you to release personally chosen
old unwanted mental traits called "Body Parts In Space".

Highly recommended are:
"A New Earth" and "The Power of Now" by Eckhart Tolle

"Home Coming - Reclaiming And Championing Your Inner Child"
by John Bradshaw

The Louis Schwartzman TED talk on Gratitude (Google it)

The many books, lectures and meditation of Swami Chetanananda

Deva and Miten - 21 Day Sanskrit Mantra Journey
http://devapremalmiten.com/884-21-day-mantra-meditation-journey

Barrie Konicov Potentials Unlimited (Audio Self Hypnosis)
http://www.potentialsunlimited.com/about.cfm Chakra balancing

Shirley MacLaine - http://www.shirleymaclaine.com/

Oprah - Super Soul Sunday.

The works of Thich Nhat Hanh

"8 Habits Of Love: Overcome Fear And Transform Your Life"
By Rev. Ed Bacon

" The Alchemist" by Paulo Coelho
"Spiritual Liberation", " Life Visioning" by Michael Bernard Beckwith

"The Seven Spiritual Laws of Success: A Practical Guide to the Fulfillment of Your Dreams" by Deepak Chopra

Caroline Myss:

http://www.amazon.com/Entering-Castle-Finding-Inner-Purpose/dp/074325533X/ref=asap_bc?ie=UTF8

"To Be Healed By The Earth" by Warren Grossman

The Beatles:
If you listen for content, many of their lyrics, especially John's, had deep spiritual meaning. The Beatles were, pardon the pun, instrumental in bringing the basic concepts of spiritual awakening to the western world.

"Resilience From The Heart: The Power To Thrive In life's Extremes"
by Gregg Braden

"A Return to Love" and "A Year of Miracles" By Marianne Williamson

Kai   Hu   -   http://www.wellbeingalignment.com/kai-hu-mission.html

199

"Huna: Ancient Hawaiian Secrets for Modern Living" by Serge King

"The Art Of Healing: Uncovering Your Inner Wisdom And Potential For Self-Healing" By Bernie Siegel

Link to one of many books by Doreen Virtue http://www.amazon.com/Angels-101-Introduction-Connecting-Working/dp/1401946038/ref=sr_1_12?s=books&ie=UTF8&qid =1458570019&sr=1-12&keywords=doreen+virtue+books

"A Course In Miracles" by The Foundation for Inner Peace https://www.amazon.com/Course-Miracles-Foundation-Inner-Peace/dp/1883360269

An introduction to "A Course in Miracles" (An Amazon search of - An introduction to "A Course in Miracles" will connect you with these books or go to: **http://www.acim.org/**

"Journey Of Souls" by Michael Newton

"Turning The Mind Into An Ally" by Sakyong Mipham (deals with meditation)

"The Disappearance of the Universe" by Gary Renard

"Easy Breezy Prosperity" by Emmanual Dagher

Michael Sealey hypnosis YouTube for positive changes to your subconscious: https://www.youtube.com/watch?v=FiPDV9L5qpQ

Carolyn L. Mein "Releasing Emotional Patterns with Essential Oils"

"How Your Mind Can Keep You Well" by Roy Masters

"Shadows Before Dawn:
Finding the light of Self-Love Through Your Darkest Times"
By Teal Swan

"One Spirit Medicine"
Ancient Ways to Ultimate Wellness
by Alberto Villoldo

"The Tapping Solution" by Nick Ortner

John Bradshaw, "Healing the Shame That Binds You"

https://mooji.org/
Mooji offers information for self discovery

Kyle Gray:
Angel Prayers: Harnessing the Help of Heaven to Create Miracles

"The Shift" DVD movie with the late Dr. Wayne Dyer

Space for your future notes:

Space for your future notes:

Space for your future notes:

This book is a spiritual primer. A springboard if you will, for anyone interested in improving themselves, their surroundings, understanding why we exist and discovering the mind's secrets to a spiritually oriented life. Had I had this book 40 years ago and was able to absorb its contents, my life would have been immeasurably easier. I would have saved years of research and been given answers for the reasons for my life's trials.

Most are not ready to believe 100% in the contents of this book, some are. If you are one of the some, I have written this for you. You and the others who can benefit from being exposed to these teachings are what this world requires in order to allow the positive growth of human consciousness to the next phase. I welcome you and am proud of you for your willingness to challenge who and what you are and for joining us on this most important of life's awakening journey.

If you are not part of the some and conclude some of the contents of this book are not valid for you at this time, that is fine. The world needs contrasts and available challenges to rise above and go beyond, in order to allow man's continued growth.

One of the main reasons for having this book in print is to leave it for future generations, as needed. I consider this work a stepping stone of sorts and with hope, it will always be available when you are ready.

Sincerely,

David A. Rench

Made in the USA
Charleston, SC
23 September 2016